It's not How, It's Why ?

For the People
Who Believe In Achieving their Dreams

Ranjit Samal

This is a work of non-fiction. Names, characters, businesses, places, events and incidents are either products of the author's imagination or used in a fictitious manner. Any resemblance to actual persons, living or dead, or actual events is purely coincidental.

First Print: July 2017
Sixth Print: July 2022
Printed in India

Printed at Brandigo Private Limited, Navi Mumbai
Typeset in Calibri

ISBN: 978-93-84180-58-4

Cover Design: Sneha, Team StoryMirror

STORYMIRROR
Stories that reflect you

Publisher:	StoryMirror Infotech Pvt. Ltd. 7th Floor, El Tara Building, Behind Delphi Building, Hiranandani Gardens, Powai, Mumbai, Maharashtra - 400076, India.
Web:	storymirror.com
Facebook:	@storymirror
Twitter:	@story_mirror
Instagram:	@storymirror
Contact Us:	marketing@storymirror.com

This books is dedicated to
all the youngsters of our nation
who believe in achieving their dreams

Acknowledgement

I am blessed with an amazing family, a fantastic team of friends and supporting colleagues who have helped me in every step of my life. These people deserve a heartfelt thanks and kind appreciation. I express my sincere gratitude to each one of them for assisting me through the pathway to my dreams.

My deepest gratitude to Dr. Radhakrishnan Pillai, bestseller author of *Corporate Chanakya* and Director of CIPL, Mumbai, for being a wonderful source of inspiration to me. His teachings provided me a lot of insight about leadership.

Genevieve Pereira, for patiently reading every line of the script and providing me instant implementable feedback.

Sakshi Sharma, Alok Asawa, Subhalaxmi Senapaty, Suyash Jain, Ankur Pandey, and Nikhil Punetha thank you for being wonderful friends to me, for always being by my side, supporting my ideas and encouraging me to fearlessly take up new challenges. Special thanks to ITM's family, especially IB batch 2012–14, for believing in my potential.

My childhood friends, Somesh Mahapatra, Manisha Mishra, Prasad Satpathy, Navjyoti Baral, Sunil Mohanty, Trupti Prakash Pattnaik, for always being my well-wishers and close to my heart. Your friendship matters a lot to me.

Thanks to Story Mirror for believing in my script and designing an inspiring cover page and then carrying out the entire publication. A big thanks to the editorial team and the designing team for making the book error-free and presentable.

Thanks Mom and Dad for blessing me and providing a "backend support." Special thanks to my Uncle Mr. Kailash Samal, who always supported me in my tough times and made me stronger to chase my dreams.

My elder brother, Mr. Ajit Samal for inspiring me, directing and supporting me with my crazy ideas.

A Deepest gratitude to Mr. Ankit Das, Mr. Ramprasad Subudhi and Mr. Prakash Sahoo for being my inspiration who showed me a strong reason to be successful.

A big thank you to all the characters of this book, who have knowingly or unknowingly inspired me, taught me and guided me to share the learnings that are featured in the book.

Finally, my gratitude, to all the readers who will be reading this book with the hope to chase their dreams with a valid purpose.

My Suggestion while reading this book

This book is practical and all about real life experiences. It will provide you with plenty of reasons to understand the importance of your dreams that lead to your success.

The entire book is based on self-realization. All the chapters are kept in order and should be read one by one. Most important, realizing the contents and the need of all concepts in your life is what one needs to do. The collective elements of this book will give rise to all the principles of success. These are very simple real-life examples that you can relate to your personal life and implement the concepts.

Use this book as a practice tool. While reading sit down with a pen and dairy, and start making your own notes. Try to answer the self-answered questions given at the end of some chapters. Introspect yourself. What are the skills and knowledge you need, to be a better performer in every area of your life? Find out the answers, discuss with your partner, parent, mentor, or close friends. Start giving plenty of reasons to yourself, that why do you want to succeed in each and every area of your life?

While reading the book you can find out all the reasons for your life from specific concepts related in this book. By the time you complete this book, your practice book itself will be the reason for survival and intense hard work. I am sure if it is done with dedicated concentration it could turn into your autobiography. All the best!

Contents

It's for You!

I was eighteen. I had everything that a student could wish for:

A good scholastic education.

Good grades and records.

Prizes, certificates and trophies in sports.

Yet a dream to be an IITian never got fulfilled. I enrolled myself with CV Raman Institute for B. Tech, which turned out to be the best four years of my life.

A dream to start something of my own was finally fulfilled. I started selling door to door e-learning products. I grew, excelled and became independent before my 20s. As I was travelling across the entire state for business promotions, I not only enjoyed, but also learned a lot. Unfortunately, I was not able to be super successful. Everything broke.

Why did I do all this? Why did all this happen? I was shattered. Nothing went according to my expectations. Yet I believed, the almighty had something better in store.

Again, a dream to be an IIM graduate never got fulfilled. I joined ITM B-School, Mumbai, to complete my master's degree. I hated taking up a job and working under a boss. I tried searching for some like-minded people at my workplace, with whom I could share my thoughts but all in vain!

More than my classmates, I found the library more compatible to cater to my thoughts. I entered the premises before everyone and left after dusk. To utilize my time and get over boredom, I decided to write down all the lessons that I had learnt in my early life.

Days passed by, concepts kept on adding in my journal and the pages touched hundred. I was immersedin my thoughts --"Why was I not successful in the past?" I tried to find suitable answers for "How to be successful?" to convince myself. I went through each and every row and column of the library, searched each and every shelf, and read and re-read books.

Finally, I endedup being so confused with the different theories, concepts, directions and solutions that boasted about being successful, that I forgot to ask myself "Why be successful?" instead of "How to be successful?"

I decided to touch on "Why?" before I enter "How?" to be successful. All my life lessons connected automatically when I steadily triggered "Why be successful?"

My reasons and purpose becameconcrete, ideas matured and plans got fixed, to come up with a book for the youth to give them reasons to be successful but with a different angle – connecting the principle of success.

That's the first book "It's not "how", its "why"

"Life always Survives with a Reason"

After I finished engineering, deciding to take a diversion from the field of technical studies, sounded like a crazy idea, specially after spending 4 precious years of my life on it. It was an intense personal decision to explore the field of my interest – where the real job of life sounded challenging. My passion lay in the field of "Business innovations" i.e. innovating new business ideas, creating directions for revenue source, finding solutions to any business strategy. An area where I felt I could explore my abilities.

Understanding business is more or less like understanding human minds. Everything happens for a reason, be it personal success, corporate growth or a nation's development. Understanding each and every theory related to the same and converting them into a book was not planned.

I swear I'd never thought of writing a book.

But I guess, I did it: the funniest and craziest part of my life. Thank you for picking "It's not how, It's Why". This book is for you.

Youngsters, who believe in their dreams and are really passionate about achieving them, can get insights from here. Understanding the value of a REAL dream, the power of belief, the magic of positive attitude, being a self-made man, leading life with leadership, thinking out of the box and being a mirror for one's success are certain reasons which have helped people to be successful in society and at the same time not losing yourself is what the book tells you about.

Pardon me, but now that you are reading the book, I must admit that I didn't actually come up with the idea of writing theories, but it is here because it was destined.

Most of us are dismayed bythe lessons life teaches us.

It's a real-life experience which ignited me to share my thoughts with you all.

Recalling my second-year engineering days, I got to know about an electronic gadgets exhibition to be held in our city. Some famous personalities from various electronic industries were invited to be the speakers for the inauguration event. I was lucky enough to collect an entry pass for the event from one of my friends. Irrespective of the experience I would gather, I decided to visit the venue. On the day of the event, my friend who was supposed to join me was not able to make it due to some personal reasons. I decided to go alone.

It was 7 pm in the evening. After completing my sales follow-up and interacting with some negative customers, I reached the venue just in time. As soon as I reached the premises, the security guard closed the door. I realized that I was the last person to enter the well-decorated entrance gate. "It was my day!" I exclaimed. The seminar consisted of a huge crowd and majority of them were youngsters. As I headed towards the seminar, I felt motivated looking at the entire setup in front of me. There were famous personalities from different electronic gadget companies sitting on the stage as guests of honor. I carefully heard the speech made by some senior executive of an electronic gadgets company. His speech was wonderful and inspiring.

Previously, I had attended many seminars and motivational events by well-known personalities including famous businessmen, youth entrepreneurs, CEO's and chairmen of well-known companies. I had heard a lot of success stories from other events too but that day was different. It was special. Strikingly different from the success stories I had heard previously. I was able to feel the real transformation in my thoughts. Even though it was cold, I could feel the warmth of my breath continuously encouraging me, triggering positive thoughts about myself. My entire focus was on the words of the speaker. His presentation skills and the way he addressed the crowd made me feel more positive. It was more of a déjà vu.

He spoke about his dreams; the efforts he had put in to

reach where he was currently. The endeavors, initiatives and the innovations he made to enhance the company's profits. His words about innovations and dedication towards his organization ignited my dreams and made me realize "Why not me, too?" I couldn't stop imagining myself standing at the podium, addressing a similar crowd and sharing my experiences and achievements with them. I promised myself, that one day I would achieve such success. I would become a public figure.

Someone has rightly said "The two most important days in your life are, the day you are born and the day you find out why". I decided to focus on the latter ; "The day you find out why".

I wanted to have a heart-to-heart conversation with the speaker. I wanted to hear him more. I was anxious. I waited till the end of the event to get a chance to meet him personally. Sneaking through the tight security arrangement, I tried to reach him personally and ask about the secret of his success and his achievements. As soon as the event got over I rushed towards him to take a chance to greet him personally. He was a tall man with wheatishcomplexion. He was formally dressed with a pair of grey color glasses that merged well with his personality. The charm of success was easily noticeable. A vibration of richness was in the air. My heart thumped hard, the adrenaline rush activated my senses, and energized me to ask a simple question. "Sir, how did you achieve all this success?" He paused and looked at me with a surprise. I was afraid of the security and the criticism of the general crowd. I was expecting some real-world solution, with some rocket science concepts and mixed with some angular measurement of Pythagoras theorem. The answer I received from him was really surprising. With a smiling face, and composed disposition, he answered –

"I don't know how I'm successful, but I always wanted to be successful and so I am".

That's it, and he left. The security guard pulled me out, and I got lost in the crowd. I came aside from the crowd which was busy in waving and shaking hands with all the dignitaries. I wondered about the simple answer I got from him. I went back home and kept on thinking about it the entire night. How was it possible that without knowing he was successful, he became successful? I wondered if he had mocked my query. His simple comment that he always wanted to be successful and today he is, boggled my mind like a puzzle that needed to be solved.

I was repeatedly murmuring his words the whole night. I lay wide awake until it was dawn. The sunbeams raided in from the eastern window. His words still rang in my ears. My question was unanswered. What made that person successful and what is the meaning of "he always wanted to be successful and he is?" Months passed by and I was still looking for a concrete answer to my query. It took a lot of time to understand the meaning of those sentences in depth. I have come across some leadership gurus, and successful personas – some dynamic, energetic, curious, ambitious youths, men and women who love their life a lot. They work for their dream and fight till they achieve it. I analyzed and even realized a lot regarding the success parameter from these life teachers. After some intense interaction and personal research, I came to know that "life depends on its purpose for living and solid reasons to carry forward life effectively." A purposeful life is always a better and self-directed life.

The speaker was a successful person because he was very clear about this reason to be successful i.e. why he wanted to be successful, and "how" to be successful just followed "why". Our life needs reasons and these reasons lead to the events and incidents that take place in our life, and probably thus leading to success. The moment our reasons are clear and we are headstrong about it, we are close to being 'successful.'

Whenever we face tough situations in life, we have to take a decision, make a commitment, set goals, etc. These ideologies help us to determine our way towards success. Purpose in an individual's life is the only way to success, if an individual has the purpose; it becomes easy for him to achieve the success he desires. If your purpose is clear, then no matter what the situation would be, you are going to fight till you succeed. Every principle of life and success comes into play if you are clear with your "WHY". Your action plan, your attitude, your leadership skills, your learning curve and every possible principle for success will come into play very effectively.

I am not a professional writer; neither did I have any intention to write any books. A childhood dream of becoming an aeronautical engineer and designing aircrafts was replaced withbecoming a computer science engineer. Then I landed up being a management professional and a youth educator.

Since I was 17, I was involved in doing part time jobs and short-term business ventures. Along with my studies I was passionate about earning money. Right from my engineering days, I believed that life is a onetime gift and I will live every moment. Life is a celebration and I have to make it successful to celebrate each and every second of it. It's a do-it-yourself-project.

Once I was visiting Pal Heights, one of the premium shopping malls where some of my associates, very young and equally passionate about living their dreams, came to meet me for a discussion. After the discussion was over, one of them from the group stayed back and requested me for some additional time. I was expecting some queries related to business. True to my intuitions, I was bombarded with some sales queries. Our discussions varied from sales strategies to training events. Post discussion, I realized his purpose of requesting me for extra time was a reason that surprised me completely.

He told me "Sir ji, there are many associates and youth who are learning from your conferences. Your words are really inspiring and have helped a lot in our city. Why don't you take it ahead and pen them down?" I was taken aback. I relished the idea that people do expect a lot from me. I'm a person who is very passionate about learning new things. Certain emotions literally forced me to write down all my thoughts and feelings. That day I wondered why not write a book! If not for everyone, I could write it for myself! My future could read it. There are a lot of people who believe in me, and expect a lot from me. All the lessons I have learnt should be recorded. This book replicates the real-life incidents and teachings that connect principles of success and gives a new dimension to understanding why you have to be successful.

This book, "It's Not How, It's Why" contains the top nine valuable reasons that make one successful and most importantly, why one has to be successful? This is completely youth-focused. What makes one keep going towards success? What are certain self-questions a youth should ask? What should be the thought process of a youth? A youth's dream, his personal belief, the ability to lead, a proper attitude are certain parameters which strengthen one's mindset to live a purposeful life. Today's youth are tomorrow's inspiration and they should create a culture of setting a benchmark through breakthrough innovations and living their passion with proper intentions.

Why should one be successful? Is money, a large house, a luxury car, a great lifestyle, popularity, high extent of political reach the only reasons that attract people? Is it that one has to be successful for one's own self? Yes! These are the primary reasons which motivate the crowd to be successful. In today's world of competition, growing business innovations and also keeping in mind the level of corruption, we are in an intense requirement of implementing values and principles of life and most importantly understanding the societal and personal needs to be a successful personality. The nine aspects mentioned below will connect us to understand why one has to be successful, primarily covering personal, family, society and taking nation into consideration.

- You have to be successful because there is a real want to achieve in your life. Life is a fight between "you" and "what you want". The moment you stop fighting for what you want, what you don't want will automatically take over. This leads to frustration and dissatisfaction. Achieving the **'Real want'** will give you a pure feeling of being successful.

- You have to be tagged as a **'Self-made man'**, a man of honor. One who stands as a one-man army, to contribute your potential for societal development.

- There's a demand for you to be successful, to attract people who want to be successful. An intentional thought will align your activities to meet like-minded people and to help them in their path of success, thus the thought recognized as a **'Fruitful thought'**. The power of your feelings, love, and gratification will always be a source to make others successful and that starts from your intentions to be successful.

- The importance of your words, the value of your ideas and your existence should make an impact in society. People should believe you, and for that you have to be labeled as a successful personality, in turn to achieve that, you should believe the work you are doing, the system you are associated with and most importantly a strong **'Belief'** in yourself.

- The society you belong to, the crowd who knows you, should understand the real value of the attitude you carry. A vibration of **'Meaningful attitude'** in you should teach the audiences. Everyone should accept you as an influential positive entity and for that you have to be stamped with the term 'a successful one'.

• Your visions, values and achievements should be a benchmark and that's what society nowadays, especially the youth, are searching for. There's a need for you to be positioned as a **'Leader'** and being successful will follow the same.

• Need, want, results and achievements are a never-ending process. A new benchmark can be set and achieved by proving ourselves in our society. You have to be successful because there's a next big thing waiting for you. **'Thinking big'**, working for it and achieving it should inspire the audiences to think bigger. Every success story starts with proper intention and your influential intention will inspire others to think big and for that you have to be a successful figure.

• You have to be successful because you failed someday. You have an inspiring story to tell the universe – the learning from failure, the implemented lessons and the situation you turn around to be a successful one is always waiting to be shared in public. Your failure is always a **'Positive failure'** and to share that, there's a need for you to be a successful person.

• You will be a mirror for others. People should see you as an idol. They should follow you, learn from you and make you their mentor. For that, you have to be successful and constantly become a **'Mirror to yourself'**, grow consistently and create records by achieving your 'Real Want'.

1

The Real Want

"The indispensable first step to getting the things you want out of life is this: decide what you want."- Ben Stein

How are the rich differentiated from the poor? How does success differ from failure? What makes a person famous? How to create a positive environment? How can a dreamer be different from the rest? When I came across the words 'dreams' and 'goals', I started to examine my own conscious thoughts. To my surprise, it gave me leverage to think deeply about every aspect of my life. I became more focused on converting my dreams into reality.

This was a life-changing experience.

I call these dreams and goals as **'The Real Want'**.

What according to you could be the reasons behind being successfully rich and famous? Is it because they are lucky, working too hard or being smart? Did they master that particular field or are exceptionally talented? That's not 'how' people like Mahatma Gandhi, Dhirubhai Ambani, Bill Gates, and others are famous. So 'why' are they rich and famous? That is the moot question. These personalities were not born famous or in rich families, but they were very confident and focused on what they wanted in their life and why they wanted it in their life.

Mahatma Gandhi's, experimentation with truth, shows that he knew the meaning and significance of independence and why was it the most important need. Once the concept of "why" was completely clear, he had hundreds of reasons for his struggle to fight for the freedom of our nation.

I was the type of guy who stayed out of the house most of the time. Somehow or the other, I kept wandering out of the house either to play cricket or just roam around with friends. Since childhood I enjoyed exploring the world outside – discovering new ideas and connecting every idea to a source of revenue generation fascinated me most. Home for me was a library when I wanted to study – integrating and differentiating my homework by experimenting with the principle of Archimedes, numerical of Newton's law and with a constant focus on optics, had always tempted me to spend a longer time with subjects like mathematics and physics. Home for me was a centre, where the hungry me was fed with love and care of my mother, a place where I enjoyed quality evenings with my family and friends.

Life took a turn when I shifted to Bhubaneswar, the temple city of India, for completing my engineering degree. Being away from home and family, in a city with completely unknown people, was in itself a prodigious experience. Life seemed to be thrilling and exquisite. The feeling of being independent was fabulous. That was the phase when I learned some of the important lessons of my life. The meaning of life, understanding my real want, definition of success for me, the importance of a value-based admired family, imperative of self-analysis, etc. are the certain advocacies that I received from my experiences.

In Bhubaneswar, I used to stay in a government guest house with one of my childhood friends- Prem Tarash. Just like his name, Prem is always admired and loved by all. He was the most helpful guy I had ever come across. A tall and thin guy with a height that touched our room's entrance, he had crinkle hair, and a glass always at the tip of his nose. Prem was always ready to help everyone who asked for help. Our friendship had always been with strong co-operation. Concentrating on my technical studies, attending classes in the first half of the day and focusing on my part-time business ventures in the second half became my daily routine. As time passed by, I started enjoying my engineering life. Prem was an influential part for our enjoyment. From nights out to riding bikes and exploring the new city became a part of our everyday activities. The thrill of escaping the police vans and patrolling cars during our nights out, were the moments I cherish the most.

I used to stay near the Central Reserve Police Force (CRPF) square. It had a big marketplace which was always crowded till midnight. In the evening, the square blushed with light and soft musical refrain. Young couples across the streets were adding glamour to the place. In this beefy crowd, somewhere in the corner of the footpath stood a "Thela wala bhai" who sold "Bhel Puri". Prem and I were his regular customers.

Most of the days before we went back to our room, we would eat "Bhel Puri" from him. It was not the Bhel puri that attracted me to go there, but his charm and welcoming attitude. Whenever I visited his stall, I noticed that every time he sold a plate, he took out a paper from his account box and put a tick mark across it. I never paid heed to that, thinking it might be something related to his daily sales but somewhere at the back of my mind it was always a big suspense.

I still remember the day, 3rd August 2007 when I found out the secret of the paper. As usual we went to the Thela in the evening for Bhel Puri. Like every day, as soon as he sold a plate, he took out the same paper and put a tick mark. I noticed the same again but didn't dare to ask him about it. So I just ate my stuff and returned. I was still curious about the unusual practice. That night, we set out on our scooty to explore the city. It was around 1 am. We decided to have tea and since it was late night, the only option was the railway station tea stall. On our way, back from the station after having tea we happened to see our "Thela wala bhai". I was surprised when I saw him. It was 2 o' clock. I was not aware of the fact that he was still selling his stuff, at this time of the hour, on the station. I wondered why he was selling Bhel puri so late into the night.

I wanted to know more about him. What made the man work so hard? He was somewhere in his mid-30's. Although he had a shabby appearance, his eyes spoke a lot. His eyes were filled with fortitude, passionate enough to achieve something big. I couldn't resist my temptation. Curiously, I moved close to him and asked him about this unusual hour of his business.

He replied, “Saab, today’s sheet was incomplete so I thought of doing night shift”.

“Sheet”? I asked. I had an idea what he was talking about, but now I mustered the courage to ask him everything, in detail.

(His face was full of sweat, his eyes focusing on my retina, lips vibrating with the fear of critique. I was expecting him to ignore my words. Hesitantly, he showed me the sheet of paper consisting of some 30 points.)

“This paper Saab”, he said; “it has a list of the reasons for my life and the reasons for doing this business. Whenever I make a sale and feel that I have fulfilled one of these reasons, I put a tick mark against it. Today my list was incomplete. All my reasons were not fulfilled so I thought of coming to the station with the hope that my list will be completed here”.

I was thrilled, it was a lesson learnt indeed. Feeling a positive resonance to his story, I felt motivated and refreshed. After he completed his story, Prem and I looked at each other trying to find words to restart the conversation and to know more about the contents of the paper. Without any further lead to our conversation, we both ordered another plate of Bhel Puri from him. Satisfied, we made our way back.

After returning to our guest house, I mulled over the lesson learnt from the Thela wala bhai and recalled the list he had shown me. It was about his “Dreams and Goals”. His reasons and goals for life were pellucid. He was passionate about them and could even work through the night to realize them. I actualized the internal meaning and initiation of his passion. It was his reason for survival. Honestly, it was not ‘how” he would do such hard work; rather it was ‘Why’ should he do such hard work.

The most important aspect in our life is to have a vision and to decide, what we really want from our lives. A purposeless life is a useless life. A person without a real want always remains confused in his activities, dissatisfied with life; he often gets surrounded with futile and worthless activities, which never leavea positive impact on his life. One has to be very clear about what one wants from all the areas of life – materialistic, education, relationship, society, finance, etc.

It was around 3 a.m. that night. Lying wide awake on my bed I thought about the man selling Bhel puri. The lesson I had learnt from him, was indeed a valuable one. My thoughts changed, my intentions towards my life got modified. I could visualize my reasons for survival in all aspects of life. I was so inspired that I went to the desk, picked up my dairy and started jotting down my reasons for survival. How would I strive to achieve success in the next few years? What should be my status? What do I need to do for my parents, family, society? What should be my contribution towards our nation? How would I like to see myself in personal and professional life? What should be my values and basic beliefs?

I started analyzing my life from every dimension. Every aspect was introspected, and I tried to figure out the reasons for my survival, my dreams and my goals. Connecting deeply with my inner self and its wants, I was immersed in visualizing the future I wanted to live. A feeling of satisfaction vibrated through my thoughts. I was happy and relaxed. Every breath I took was mixed with the feeling of enthusiasm and gratitude. I did not realize it was already dawn until the guard knocked on the door as a morning call.

It was 7 o'clock in the morning. It took me around 4 hours to prepare my list. I came up with 81 points covering almost all aspects of my life. As I held the reasons for my survival, I got a direction to go ahead in my life. It was the blueprint of my life and success. I was quite energetic and since that day, ceaselessly and tirelessly, I started working hard towards realizing those dreams and goals.

Throughout my engineering days, I worked day and night to achieve my targets. I conducted surveys and asked people about their dreams and aspirations - interacting with successful businessmen, youth entrepreneurs, social activists, leadership gurus, spiritual leaders, daily workers and street vendors; it included almost everyone I met. Why is dreaming important? How are people with concrete dreams able to change their life? The interactions succeeded with plenty of solutions that I was looking for.

We are all unique and have different thought process; this thought process leads to the creation of our dreams. These are the

'Real Wants' in our lives and the most important aspects of our survival - In the sense of name, fame, satisfaction, happiness, peace and the category of ultimate priority. Whether rich or poor everyone works hard to realize their ambition, and dreams. The poor farmers toiling in the fields have different dreams and ambitions compared to the corner office fellow in his air-conditioned comfort. A poor man works exhausted day in and day out to fulfill his basic daily needs, yet sometimes he fails, while a rich man gains wealth and fame with the same amount of commitment. The difference lies in their Real want, differentiating their priorities and the passion to chase them.

"People are differentiated on the quality of their thought process and the passion to chase their Real Want"

During my late teen years, I discovered and realized that the real wealth of life is not money, but it is time. I may earn a million till I die, but not being able to utilize it at the time of my need is baseless. My motto should be, I earn and I live. Dreams are meant for all and it's essential to be achieved at the right phase of life.

Real want – a fear factor for losers:

Many people fear to dream because they think, big dreams need money to be fulfilled. A dream to have a luxury car, a dream to opt for higher education, a dream to create a passionate business or own a dream house, everything requires money to fulfill. But trust me, there are people, who have achieved everything out of nothing. They have started from scratch and have created castles. Unfortunately, the truth lies in the fact that the reason behind the fear is not the lack of money but the constant efforts and dedication required to fulfill those dreams. Uninterrupted efforts, steady commitment, devotion towards the real want and the ability to adapt according to any situation are quite crucial. Many of us don't want to change and mould ourselvesin order to achieve our Real Want over a period of time – welcoming change in terms of accepting new skills, taking calculated risks, being with the present economy and market, adapting to technological changes and certain changes in spiritual thoughts. This disinclination to change turns into a misguided sense of fear. This fear and inability to change always gives rises to an excuse for lack of money. A dream doesn't require money to fulfill it, but a constant focal point should always be to achieve "The Real Want".

"It's not the fear of "lack of money", rather the inability to work for the dream"

People who lack confidence, often tend to back out even if a little effort could have helped them to achieve their dreams. The "I-am-ineligible" attitude always indulges a negative belief which often lands intoan unsuccessful and unhappy life. Why should one be afraid to dream? If you dream, you are halfway successful. You dream because you want it. So instead of being afraid, if you really want it, be ready to work hard and achieve it. People, who fear to dream big, are the ones who are not ready to work for it. Dreaming without purpose is a foolish dream. Your dream should have plenty of reasons to convince your own self; based on these reasons you can create an action plan to fulfill it. Dream to achieve those, not just for the sake of dreaming.

The real value of your dreams:

Not only should one harbor dreams to be successful and rich, to own a big house, a luxurious car, but also work hard to achieve it. During the phase of fulfilling your dreams you may face many failures. Treat them to be lessons you need to learn. Every time you fail, learn from it. Don't give up. Keep practicing and you can increase your potential. Remember, practice makes a man perfect. In the process, you learn to value your dream. Your inner satisfaction comes from the enlightenment of your mind and the knowledge you have gained; this is what we achieve as a lesson from our learning curves. The most important lesson I have learnt is that, once we are very clear about our Real want, we should commit ourselves to achieve it. A dream can't be a fuel for life, just a passing interest and not a real one.

Consider these thoughts as your own:

I want to own a big house.

I have a big house of my own and I'm happy to live in it.

Which of the two do you think is more effective? The first one is more interested in having the dream. Whereas, the latter makes you feel accomplished about your achievement! Isn't it?

He feels proud and happy to own it. As per the survey most of the people in society belong to the "Interested" category. So, the difference lies between feeling your dream, rather than being interested in it. People with real dreams are always committed to achieving them.

I usually get motivated after reading books. I was always interested in writing a book of my own - expressing my thoughts, beliefs and intentions towards the society in a form of a book. It never really happened until this interest began changing and I started to feel my dream. Whenever I read any book, I felt as though it were my own book. I pampered any book I saw, I took care of it, and kept it well-protected. I was in love with my dream. Books became my top priority.

The fact is that when I converted my interests into "Real Want", my perception toward a particular thing changed - the sense of belonging, the feeling of possessing, and the vibration of positives towards the book changed. I remember the evening when I committed myself to writing a book. Since then my priority got a direction. I started researching, interacting with different kinds of people who helped me to find answers to the questions that went into writing this book. Practically speaking, it took me a year to publish this and I'm happy that you are reading it.

"When you are interested in doing or achieving something, you only do it when it is convenient, but when you are committed to doing something you accept no excuses, only result is what you deserve and achieve"

Why should we have a dream? I interacted with friends, family, relatives and college mates, to understand their dreams. The phase of interaction, discussion and understanding, the thought process of people around me further impelled me to write this book. People think dreams are limited and restricted. I would differentiate them in different categories:

Dreamers with limited dream:

Belonging to an engineering background, I realized that the most perfect words to describe an engineer should be notoriously creative. I have met many people from different religious and cultural backgrounds and through interaction with them I enlightened myself about their dreams and aims. What exactly do they aim forin their life? As expected, I got typical answers as an engineer demands – to work in an MNC and earn a good package. Then what else? The usual litany: good life, a beautiful wife, two kids and so on.

The dreams were limited to getting jobs! What next? People often limit their dreams due to the family background they belong, their society, lack of motivation and other external issues. No matter what the external factor may be, if a person is really serious about his dreams and is committed, nothing can stop him from achieving that. Achieving your dream comes later, but dreaming and being clear about what you can achieve according to your potential is

the first step. Without proper thinking and planning no path can be successful, people conclude that they are not capable of fulfilling their dreams. Some even end up thinking that dreams are mere fantasy and reality doesn't exist. These are the people with "Limited dreams"

Dreamers who end up with their first dream:

One of my childhood friends was very talented and excelled in academics. He always scored good marks in our class. He was a role model for many of my classmates. He was an example for my family. He had set benchmarks for us. My parents used to inspire me to study by giving his example. I always tried to learn from him so that I could top at least once in class. But all in vain, I never succeeded. He continued his winning streak right up to the degree courses. As I was inspired by him, I once asked him, what he really wanted in life, what was his dream? His answer didn't vary, he too wanted to be an engineer and work with an MNC.

His constant dedication and intention of working in a big MNC was fulfilled. Today, he is working with a well-known MNC and earning a handsome salary. However, during my last conversation with him, he told me that he'd become an engineer, but was not happy with his life. He missed a lot of things in his life. He's become what he wanted, he is quite successful and happy in his life – but ended up without any further dream.

Dreamers with Next Targets:

I always liked to be the kind of dreamer who keeps dreaming without stopping. I have seen people who have set a goal, a target to achieve, prepared roadmaps and work hard to achieve them within a time frame. Once the target is achieved, they see a new dream – "The next Real want"- the next level for success, and work towards it with full of passion and with the same magnitude of dedication theyhad for the previous one. This type of people are never satisfied with a single dream – they are hungry for success, passionate about achievement, and have an intentionto bring about change in society. They literally create a positive vibration of success in their vicinity. They set examples and create new records. Every new dream has a process which we work on; and fulfilling these dreams helps us to grow on a regular basis through new experiences.

"A true dreamer is never satisfied, they always see a new dream – The next Real want"

Dreamers without action:

If not "this"; then 'that'. If not 'east' then 'west', If not X Ltd then Y Ltd Company, If not Monday then Thursday. This category thinks when they have a dream but doesn't make any action plan for it. They want things to happen magically, with little or almost no effort from them. I have hardly ever heard about this category fulfilling what they dreamt about. Their dreams only remain in their dream world throughout the process.

Once you are clear with what you want, and particularly why you want it, the actions phase should come into action. Your level of effort should match the intensity of your dream. If your dream is to have a BMW of your own, but your efforts are equal to buying a motorcycle, there is no meaning to your dream. You will never ever fulfill your dream. The higher your dream is, the stronger should be your plan of action for it. The best way to achieve your dream is to be very passionate about the action you are taking. The beauty of achieving dreams lies, in putting hard work for it.

"The level of your effort should match the level of your dream"

Dreaming without action is useless, actions without relevant goals and reasons are also aimless. But dreaming with focus and taking relevant action is something that will give the real satisfaction to one. Nobody will remember how fast you work; people will only remember how well you work. Thinking about your dream won't lead to success until you work hard to achieve it.

The Real Want:

During the first few days of my professional work I was told to write about my dreams. It was the time that I came to know the meaning of having a dream in mind and writing about it on a piece of paper. It was an extremely satisfying experience. I was introspecting deeply,imagining and visualizing my dreams for almost an hour or two. Imagining the beauty of my dreams and the feeling of achieving them was a heavenly experience. I was told about the miracles that happened when we express and write down our dreams on a piece of paper. The true feelings of the "Real Want" flowed throughme when I implemented it. It is scientifically proven that more than half of your work is done, once you express you dream on a piece of paper. It helps you to understand the dream as a REAL want. What is the REAL want?

R – Realistic

E – Effective

A – Achievable

L – Lifetime

Write down your dreams, as if you are living them in reality. Don't dream something which is unrealistic and absurd in nature like "I dream about walking on the ocean", "I dream about smoking cigarettes and booze with my friends on the moon". Every dream should be respected but a realistic dream acts as a motivator –it shows a valid direction to carry forward with a concrete action plan.

Don't try to cheat yourself by dreaming about something which is illogical or ridiculously stupid. By doing so, you are wasting a part of your valuable time and energy. Concentrate on those which are realistic and can be achieved.

This will direct you to keep going on your plans.

The dream should be practically action-oriented and "effective" in nature. The REAL want should be a defining factor of your survival. Understand that "Dreaming without action is useless, actions without relevant goals are also aimless." Your REAL want should be followed by a strong implementation plan to make it more effective. Any dream only kept in the mind or on a piece of paper is not an effective dream. It should be strongly executed. A big dream without execution will come alive only in the pages of your diary. The list you made should be something you want in your life anyhow. You should be ready to put in all the hard work needed to achieve it. It should not lose its shine on the way towards success. It should be concrete and have a hold on your mind till you achieve it. Your execution of the plan should dominate everything else to make the dream a REAL one.

"Remembering the Bhel puri wala, he was quite serious about the implementation of his dreams. He too had the his list of dreams written on paper, but also was ready to work until achieved."

How long will it take to achieve your dream? How long will you put in efforts to achieve "The Real Want"? What should be the "lifespan" of your dream? Defining the lifespan or the duration for the dream to be achieved is quite focused in nature. Firstly, while you are preparing your list, you should realize what your dreams are and how important they are to you. Many people find it difficult to realize what they want. It is not that people don't dream. Everyone does. It is just that they are too lazy to sit, think and write down their dreams.

Secondly, once you are clear with the list of your Real wants, you have to find out how long will it take for you to achieve them. Define a time and you need to put your efforts to achieve your dreams. Describe them in terms of days, months or years. Try to fix it within a defined time limit.

A "REAL Want"

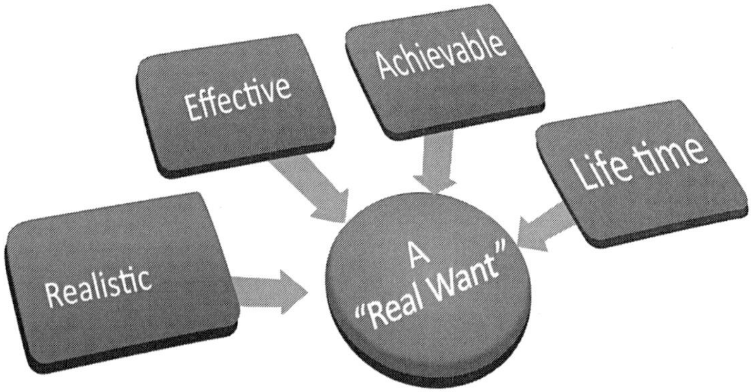

Let us differentiate between the below sentences to understand how to prepare your own list of dreams:

1. "I want to have a luxury car"
2. On 4th Oct of next year, I have booked a black BMW luxury car worth INR 60, 00,000 and I'm happy about it.

The former sentence is a REAL dream. But the latter sentence is very specific and descriptive. It is realistic and sounds convincing. It mentions a specific time span, a specific color, a specific brand. Making the dream effective varies from one person to another. It depends on the dedication towards achieve it. The REAL want is all yours. You should have a practical approach and be clear about every area of your dream.

Sit down somewhere alone; be with yourself for some time. Try to reflect on your Real want. What do you need to do to really make it beautiful? Your real want may be something materialistic, a relationship you want in your life, something you may want for your near and dear ones, higher education you want to pursue, any positive intention towards the society or the nation, a bank balance you desire, or whatever it may be. Don't pre-judge your ability to achieve, don't impose limits on your thoughts. It's a good practice to write down the dreams from each and every area of life, and that too in present tense – as if you have already achieved it and enjoying it now. It gives a positive feeling about the thing that you want and works as a game changer. In later chapters, we will see how these concepts works.

Now close your eyes and imagine a cricket match without any wickets and boundary line. What is the target of the bowler without the wicket and for the batsman without the boundary line? They are target less. Hence have a serious target and prepare a concrete action plan to achieve it. Start implementing the plan, and surely you will be differentiated.

Have a dream; make it thoroughly effective, put a constant focus on it. These are the first reasons for being a successful person. Honestly, it is not how they become successful, what efforts they put in, what kind of plan they make are not as important as the primary factor like why they want to work hard and put in those constant efforts. It is because of their dream, their values and particularly the reason to achieve – it keeps one committed till the dream is achieved. Life is a fight between "you" and 'what you want". The moment you stop fighting for what you want, what you don't want will automatically take over. This leads to rise in frustration and you are dissatisfied with your life. Achieving the **"Real want"** will give you the feelings of satisfaction and bliss. You have to be successful because you have clarity about the real want you need to achieve.

Summary

- The only thing that will ever differentiate you from the other is your "The real want."
- People who generally fear to dream are the people who are not ready to work for it.
- Dreams without a purpose or specific reason are foolish dreams.
- The lesson a person learns in the process of achieving a dream is the real value of the dream.
- There is always a difference between dream and interest.
- A dream can't be the fuel for life if that dream is not a real dream, but just an interest.
- When you are interested in achieving something, you only do it when it is convenient but when you are committed to doing something, you accept no excuse; only result is what you desire.
- There are people who have a limited dream and some who end up with achieving only their first dream.
- There are dreamers who dream, implement, achieve and dream for the next stage.
- Dreams without action and actions without dreams, both are useless.
- Your level of effort should touch the level of your dream.
- Your dream should be a REAL dream.

The Real Want: Self-answered section:

- What do you want to be known for and how would you want people to know you? Search within your mind and heart and write a page about it.
- Write down a minimum of five events, achievements, or happenings which when achieved, will make you and your parents happy.

2

A Self-Made Man

"Self-reliance is the only road to true freedom, and being one's own person is its ultimate reward"

– Patricia Sampson

Most people live a very tedious life –with similar experiences, limited success, monotonous activities, and mediocre status. As differentiated between the wealthier and the needy, mindsets and intensions can be differentiated on the similar note. During my research activities, I was lucky enough to get in touch with numerous rich and powerful people and spend quality time with them. Some of them included my friends and relatives. The interactions with them were always a part of my research activities

– understanding the human psychology, behaviors and their mindsets. After observing such people really closely, I realized that they were rich and famous not because of the quantity of money they earn or the education degree they achieved, but because of the values they carry – the decision they take, understand the learning curve and the real-life experiences they welcome. They never aspired to become rich by making money, rather they always desired to be rich in terms of knowledge, quality, attitude and their mindset – thus money followed them. On the other hand, when I glanced on the other side of the world, I came across questions that made me think deeply.

After more than 65 years of independence, why is our country still called a developing nation, not yet a developed one?

– Why do our youngsters in their 20s still ask their parents for pocket money for their basic needs?

Why even after quality education, our youngsters dream about working for MNCs, whereas youngsters in developed nations dream of owning their own venture?

– Why only a minor population earns major fraction of money?

– Why is our nation yet to solve the problem of unemployment? While these questions troubled my working hours, the answers I finally concluded with have startled me. The answers were all around me, for more than a decade. I was the one who failed to see, rather, I had ignored them, probably was not able to acknowledge it. The answer was actually cinch and transparent; it was Entrepreneurship. It was all about being a self-made man

– understanding one's "real want", finding out the core potential within; implementing the resources in creating a wealthy society and being useful to others. I came up with plenty of solutions to these questions but the most momentous reason was to focus on the importance of being independent – mentally and financially.

I belong to a joint family. Since childhood, I have observed that the only source of income for our family was my father, other than the income that came from village farming. The entire family was dependent on him for survival. Over time, my father and my elder brother commenced their business that helped our family grow. I too started working and contributed a fraction of my earning towards my family. This personal experience made me think about my neighbors, relatives and friends. When I peeped into their families, I was appalled with the conclusion I drew. In our society, on an average, if one person earns, five members of that family depend on him. If the ratio is near to 1:5, then it is very obvious that a person earning fifteen thousand per month will divide the amount among his family members for their survival. Is this division of money sufficient enough for survival for an entire month in today's world? It's unmanageable. After deep analysis I concluded that, it is not possible because of the high consumption of the family members, but because of unavailability of sources of income. Even today the most qualified people sit idle due to unemployment. Then why not think of an independent venture and be an Entrepreneur? Being independent and a reason to makes others too, it's about being "a self- made man".

It is truly said that, currently our nation is in such a situation that we need, job givers not job seekers. This self-realization ignited me to start promoting entrepreneurship among the youth. There are lakhs of people searching for jobs, but very few companies are able to provide job as per a candidate's potential. How can this handful of companies fulfill our unlimited need for work?

Learning business within 20s:

People think that starting a business is very difficult – and is meant for a select crowd. Yes, it is difficult, but only if you are an amateur. Doing a business is as easy as a newborn baby learning how to crawl or start walking. A small baby, just a few months old learns how to crawl, stand on his feet, and start walking. It's a big challenge at that age. All of us have gone through this stage and so we are able to walk today. It was too difficult at that time, but we enjoyed learning how to walk. Imagine what would have happened if our moms had started teaching us how to walk 8 years after birth? There is always a right time to start everything. Similarly, there is a right time to learn and start a business. Probably there are two best ages to start a business and become successful. Once when influenced by the opportunity and the other depending upon the level of your readiness to the market.

People often set-uptheir business at the wrong age; as a result, they suffer a lot. Society points at them and blames them for failing. As a result, many of them quit while some still struggle for their success. This failure creates fear within, and buried in fear of criticism people never take the initiative to come up with innovative ideas. I have seen people employed at the top hierarchy, earning a handsome salary but the efforts they put into earning this arenot simple. They do back-breaking work which is like the one required to manage one's own venture. If the amount of work is the same, activities are mostly similar, then why aren't people interested in starting and managing their own business. I have asked this question many times to professionals working at the top level for big MNC's. What can we do now? They said. It's done, and we are earning a good amount". I was unsatisfied with their answers. How can one's potential be limited to this? How can one be satisfied within limited dreams and achievement? I asked them again. You have knowledge, ideas, experience and resources, then why don't you start your own business? Be your own boss! The answers they gave stopped me from asking any further questions. They said; "Son, I do appreciate what you are saying but I don't have time and age. This is not our age to start a business anymore and go through the struggle once again. To earn such a big amount, it already consumed one third of my life. Now at this age it is quite difficult to rebuild our own venture. Our experience, network and resources will help, but at this age we will not be able to give complete dedication to our start-ups. At this stage, with load of responsibilities – family, mortgages and with years of habits, we are less mentally prepared to risk a jump into the unknown world and start from scratch."

Many researchers agree that there is no correct age to start a business if you have new ideas and the correct mindset. It's tough to decide upon the age as the answer to the question, generates valid and strong point from both the side – young and matured. The current national scenario in terms of economic and youth mindset; it's a positive point for the youth to start their business at a younger age.

30 minutes-drive with Mr. Eastern Rich:

It was the evening just after Diwali – the festival of lights. I was 40 kms, away from Bhubaneswar, in the oldest city of Odisha

– Cuttack, lined up with some sales presentation and follow-ups. I was so engrossed with the presentation, that I almost forgot that it was midnight and I was yet to sign my professional assignment. It was fifteen minutes past midnight when everything was over and I was waiting on the highway to return. I stood all alone shivering amidst the silenceof the cold, chilly breeze. At this time of the hour the traffic flow was limited. I couldn't find any passerby. The only thought that clickedwas to reach the nearest railway station and spend the night on the platform. Standing by the highway, alone, hungry and tired,

I regretted to have stretched the presentation for so long but at the same time I reassured myself, "Whatever happens in life, happens for a good reason". With too many conflicting thoughts in mind, both positive and negative, I was waiting for someone to give me a lift to reach home.

It was around 12:35 a.m. when I saw a car heading towards the road I wanted to take. As it came closer, its round shining head light with a curvy LED focused on me. The car stopped and I requested for a lift. Before I could complete my sentence, the right-side door – behind the driver's seat was popped open for me.

"Come in!" – A voice came from the car. I hesitated initially. Although I was in desperate need of the lift, I was also very vigilant. Suddenly I noticed the logo on the driver's steering – it was an Audi, my dream car. My nervousness was taken over by the excitement of the present situation – my fear took a transition. The excitement dissolved the fear factor within me.

The person in the car was an elderly gentleman in his mid- fifties. Attired in a white suit, his thick white moustache, directed towards the sky shined in the dim street lights. With a smiling face, he welcomed me to join him.

It was an attractive invitation which I couldn't deny. The soothing instrumental music being played on the music system added to the fragrance of him being a wealthy bureaucrat. Even though I was yet to overcome my fears, his smiling face calmed my nerves and I instantly struck a conversation with him.

Nice car. You are quite lucky - it seems you own a business and are wealthy? I started.

(He laughed): Huh! Luck... Bullshit. He replied and continued. You too are among the same category of people who often tell me this. People assume luck as God's grace upon someone but I have never experienced such in my life.

(He looked at me, I nodded my head and he continued),

When a true vision is implemented within a correct action plan, the situation is bound to be successful .... That's what luck is... *(He smiled)* When intensive hard work meets the desired real-life opportunity, an imaginary success is created... That's what people call luck.

I was rewarded with a new definition of luck; I felt as if it was among one of my valuable lectures. The person seemed to be highly educated and was quite a professional. At that point of time, my thoughts were only inclined to know, how that person became such a rich man.

"Thank you, sir, you are a learned man. You look like an owner of some well-known organization," I said.

He laughed again and this time his driver too laughed at my words. I was embarrassed but he continued :-

My son! Starting your own business and being your own boss doesn't require any type of education given in schools and colleges

scholastic education. Our basic education teaches us to manage our business, not to create one. Owning a business – it's a mind of your own. It's about travelling a path that is unknown, not travelled or less travelled. The real value is when you create a value in the society you live, through your innovation and the activity you are doing.

I was attracted towards his confidence and admired the way he shared his views.

To be successful, rich and famous, we require real life experiences – that build the human attitude to create success. Such education comes only when you face a real-life situation. Learning from our failure teaches us the practical value of achievement and success – builds the attitude to resist and win. These are real life experiences that no educational institute can provide. Instead they are learnt from our life experiences. Having good academic education is very important for people like you (he pointed at me), but at the same time you should balance it with real life education. One should understand "Being a topper in class does not mean that you will be a topper in real life too"- he stressed.

"Being top of the class does not mean that you will be a topper in real life too."

(His words were quite relevant. I would recall my school days with lots of certificates, awards and achievements. I was well-versed with the theories of physics, mathematical formulas and equations of

chemistry. For instance I realized that, I was an amateur in terms of real life experiences). I was hearing him more carefully now.

"In India, parents and our education system focus more on studying hard and becoming a topper. They forget that becoming a topper in class, doesn't make them a topper in real life - he focused on it again. It has become a trend to study hard and secure good marks. Generations after generations kowtow to this rat race. Today's situations require a different approach. Undoubtedly, being a topper is a great achievement but at the same time one should keep in mind that real life does not treat you based on marks or report cards. Practically life is a house full of failures and commitments – it throws challenges that educational institutions do not prepare us to face. When challenges appear, one tries to remember the theories onewas taught in schools and colleges. However, using them in practical life itself is a challenge. Hence, unable to cope, a person quits facing challenges and accepts his failure – which in turn makes him fearful and he becomes judgmental towards himself.

"Real life is a house full of failures, commitments and challenges"

Focusing on scholastic education and at the same time teaching our youth how to face real life struggles, will prepare them to face the challenges, making them confident and bold. It is when young people have everything – strength, learning ability, potential to apply, and good relationship networks, it familiarizes the person with practical life and real-life education. *(I nodded as he continued with the same passion and enthusiasm).*

"Encourage our youth to be motivated to work part-time during studies, start their own ventures and live their passion." He said.

"Yes sir, but earning from a low age risks the time for studies, which is quite unacceptable for our family. I do work part-time, besides my engineering and I own a small venture as well, but I don't make much money out of it". - I added to his words.

"This is a wrong perception in the mindset of the youth today."

– he replied.

(I stared at him stupefied. He smiled and continued speaking)

"The initial phase of work experience is not for making money, but to understand the value of money. Early part-time work, starting a small venture will mould one to fit into the practical world. This will build values, teach humanity, and will give satisfaction from within. This satisfaction will motivate to work on a new dream. This time the dream will not be confined only to that person, but will include society and nation as well."

"Working early in life - not for money, but for values"

(His words ignited my dream. I wanted to be with him if I could. I wanted to learn the practical aspects of business from him, but there was a time constraint. I had plenty of questions. I wanted to know more about him, about his professional background, his experiences – I hoped that he would edify me more about how to frame my career as a youth entrepreneur).

"Sir, thank you so much for sharing these valuable insights with me. You inspired me a lot." *I added.*

"Welcome my son!" *he replied.*

"What exactly you do? When did you start your business?

What is your business all about?" *I enquired curiously.*

Before he could answer anything, the driver squeaked - Bananas!

"Bananas? You mean you sell bananas"? You are so rich by selling bananas" *I said astonished.*

Both laughed. I was confused. I wondered how can a person be so rich just by selling bananas.

"Yes, my son! I used to sell bananas on the railway stations, bus stands and local streets, when I was 14 years old." *He replied proudly.*

"Do you still continue to sell bananas?" *I asked*

"No! I own industries, I'm an industrialist." *he answered.*

From selling bananas to an industrialist, it sounded interesting. "How did you make it? What were your experiences during this transition period?" *I probed.*

"My father was a farmer and I was his eldest son. My parent always wanted me to study hard and be famous. I didn't have any interest in studies."

"They always pressurized me to go to school and study hard. It annoyed me and I couldn't stand it. One day the frustration was at its peak and I decided to leave the house. At the age of 14, I stole a 500 rupee note from my father's pocket and left home to make my fortune."

"I started earning by selling bananas in the city streets and railway stations. I was always looking for new opportunities. It was my passion to utilize the entire 24 hours in an effective way. I was not aware of this real-life education then and worked to earn money for my survival. I always wanted to be independent and thus not only worked from an early age but also ventured into my own business. Apart from selling bananas, I expanded to farming. My business grew and began to yield high returns. What I learnt from that experience, made me capable of understanding the values of life at a deeper level. During this period, although I met many teachers and mentors, but the best teacher was "my failure" – it gave me the real flavor of success. From being a leader, reacting positively to situations, focusing on instant implementation to win, understanding the value of relationships and a strong sense of responsibility are certain values that seeped into my life." *(He stressed)*

"I was growing day by day. (He paused and continued), enjoying all the failures that came my way and mostly the lessons from them. My interactions with people who were jealous of me were some of the most memorable incidents – facing them, taking up the challenge to prove myself not through words but actions were wonderful opportunities and it was fun. It taught me to be generous and humble."

"Being a self-made man, I was deeply in love with my dreams. I always wanted to be independent and experience the freedom of money and time. Living a life that I always wanted was my primary intention. I never like when potential people sacrifice everything they have for a decent job. People dedicate a major fraction of their life for a higher degree and work for people whom they don't even know – they sacrifice their own dream and start fulfilling other's dreams. This made me believe that people are not passionate about their dreams – people with knowledge and intellect, who could dream big, kill their dream."

"With the increase in responsibility towards family and society, my dreams were expanding day by day. I started reflecting those by expanding my business from farming to industries – I started manufacturing agricultural and food products. I started catering to the state government. My values and attitudes were respected by society and business environment *(he smiled with pride)*. Soon I realized that I was serving more than 60% of the needs of my state in agricultural and foods products – especially the biscuits industry saw a huge growth *(he specified)*."

The concept of earning by dreaming gradually became my top priority. It's not that you will earn and then you will dream for materialistic things you want; rather it's the other way around. If you dream big (pointing me) and take suitable actions, you will automatically earn more and soon can enter the elite group of luxuries. It's not about achieving; it's about dreaming effectively. Being in love with your dreams can certainly create a positive environment and atmosphere around you. This happened with me and so it can happen with you. *(I murmured– "yes it can happen with me too")*

A 'banana seller' was talking about dreams, values, passion, responsibility and leadership. I was amazed; subconsciously I was filled with gratitude towards the man who sat next to me. I was learning, recording his every word in my mind. I imagined myself comparing my present with my future, 10 years down the line. I was overwhelmed with the knowledge and experience he shared. His oration about his passion and his business made my curiosity rise with every question I asked him.

"Why did you choose a business of farming and agriculture?"

I questioned

"My passion!" *He replied.*

"Farming is my passion; I love it from the core of my heart. I love to serve by cultivation." *(he added)*

"From where did you get this business idea?" *(I continued)*

"An idea comes from requirement. When a person's potential meets society's need, a business idea is generated."

"Necessity is the mother of invention. My son!"

(He answered and extended his thoughts)

"The potential is activated when one's passion is implemented

– meaning, passion create potential which thereby meet the need to create a business. A passion can always be converted into a business opportunity."

"Most people initiate business with the objective to earn more money and become rich, but if it's not related to one's passion the satisfaction level is always hampered. Successful people follow their passion and find out an opportunity to convert that into a business. A passionate person always finds a way to do the work he is passionate about."

"I enjoy farming. I was not bothered about the surroundings, people, or other circumstances. I didn't make any excuses and my intention was to accomplish my passion. I always wanted to be better than the best in the farming industry." *(He stressed)*

"Most of the people are not able to make out what exactly they are passionate about and thus remain mediocre for the rest of their life. Passion comes from within and to attain one's goal one can do anything without excuses. When a task is done with complete passion and is converted into business, real time success is achieved and that's a self-made man."

"A passion-oriented business gives you real life satisfaction"

He seemed to be wandering in a different world holding my hands as if asking me to explore it. Selflessly he was advising a passionate youngster to do something big. I committed myself to obey and follow his words. My heart and mind echoed with his words – (He looked at me, patted my left shoulder and continued).

"Being a self-made man is being independent and creating an environment to make others independent. You can get everything in life you want, if you just help others get what they want. One of the reasons of increasing unemployment is the lack of people taking initiative to create employment. Not all people are comparable – they are different in terms of education, responsibility, and have different dreams. If someone takes the initiative and gives their full potential in creating employment, then we will no longer be scared to chase small dreams that go into the making of a people and a country." *(He smiled)*

His eyes were expecting a lot from me. I felt that he wanted me to do something – pursue my passion and be a reason of pride in society, set an example and change the mindsets of the general public. I felt contended for inspiring me to be a self-made man.

He was just about to say something, when the driver interrupted.

"Is this the square where you want us to drop you?" The driver asked and stopped the car.

CRPF square.

"Yes, that's right!" I replied.

I never realized that more than half an hour had passed and I had reached my destination. I wished to spend more time with him, to learn more about him and his experiences but time forbade.

"Thank you, Sir, for the lift and for sharing your experiences, it was a really inspiring and knowledgeable ride." *I thanked him.*

"It's my pleasure, son!" *He smiled.*

As I was about to move away, I realized that I was so engrossed in conversing with him, that I forgot to ask his name. I was near the driver's door and he was about to speed-up the car.

"Bhai, what's his name?" *I asked hurriedly.*

With a smile he replied, "Mr. Eastern Rich!" *and went away.*

I was taken aback by the name. Never before, had I heard such a name. I thought maybe because he was one of the richest men in east India. Perhaps, this is why he replied - Mr. Eastern Rich.

I walked back home which was just 10 minutes from the square. The scene kept playing in my mind.

A sense of realization triggered my conscious mind. For instance, I thought if in a family, all the potential senior members become independent, have different sources of income then it will increase the average income of the family thereby leading to a good lifestyle. The true economic development of a nation will be held in the development of thinking and lifestyle of a person. It's possible by increasing the number of independent people in our nation – thus it will lead to Incredible India.

It was his intention to be a self-made man, which made him rich. Truly it's not 'how he became rich?' Rather 'it's why he became rich?' His reason to grow rich was clear, which made him work passionately and hence, he became famous and rich. You have to be a self-made man, a man with honor to stand alone as a one-man army to contribute your learning and potential for societal development. For that you have to enter into the league of successful people.

Summary

- *Currently our nation is in a situation where we need job givers, not job seekers.*
- *Doing a business is not a matter of luck or talent, it's about learning and implementing*
- *To be successful, you need real life education apart from the scholastic education.*
- *Learning from real life experiences will help people grow.*
- *Our youth needs to maintain a balance between scholastic and real-life education.*
- *Real life is full of failures, challenges and the need for commitment to face challenges.*
- *The initial working experience is not to earn money but to know the real value of money.*
- *Converting passion into business, gives an internal satisfaction.*
- *Being a self-made man is to be independent and create the situation for others to be independent.*

A self-made man (Self-answered section)

- *Write down your plans to make yourself independent in the next six months and describe the actions you are going to take for the same.*
- *If you are independent and have your source of income, then very honestly write down the names of two persons whom you know are not independent. Fix a plan and have a meeting with those two people and help to make them independent within next 6 months. This should be your responsibility.*
- *Point out one activity you are very passionate about - something which you are ready to do without being paid. Find out ways and take appropriate steps to convert your passion into a business.*

3

A Fruitful Thought

"Change your thoughts and you change your world"
- Norman Vincent Peale

Who am I? What am I doing in this world? Where was I before my birth? What will happen to me after my death? These are very intense questions which always trigger my mind and thought process. We all are made from a single source i.e. energy. This is a concept which has always made me inquisitive to learn more about our existence, universe's existence and mostly spiritualism. From the overall concepts of how universe exists, the study of thoughts has always been one of my interests. The study of universe, awareness of quantum physics, values of our thoughts, its vibrations and frequency has always been informative to me and I always wanted to share with all my friends and everyone I know.

How can thoughts within us create our life? Knowingly or unknowingly the thoughts we have, shape our life and destiny. There are certain laws of the universe which can give everything that we want in our life. The house I want to live in, the car you want to drive, the type of partner you want to have in your life, the business you want to do and each of your dreams is going to be possible by knowing the value of your thoughts and mostly knowing how to control your thoughts and implement them. The moment I came to know about the power of the universe, I wanted to know more about it. I asked many people, I analyzed, and did intensive research. I questioned professors, researchers, philosophers, training academies, went through hundreds of books and historical research. During my talk and questionnaire session with many professionals, I learned about the awareness people generally have about the power of the universe. Some were aware about it while others reacted as if I was mad to ask such irrelevant questions. However more than 80 % of the surveyed people agreed to what I had to say.

Personal experience and introduction to these concepts remind me of a sizzling cold, dark night, in the unknown streets of Europe. The moment I realized that it was not the same street I crossed in the evening, I was panic-stricken. I had lost my way, the architecture of building and towers were different, labeling on the street was not the same it was in the evening. The leaves of the trees were reddish, street was wider and the tram tracks on the floor were designed in a curve to take a turn towards Brugel - the hostel I was looking for. That night it was not the same. I realized I was out of track. I had lost my way towards the Van Gogh hostel- where I was staying.

I was in Brussels, Belgium. During my management studies in Europe, I was on a week-long trip from Budapest to Brussels for a visit to the European Union. It was the 2nd day in the city which was completely new to me in infrastructure, culture and climate. All my classmates distributed themselves and stayed in two hostels: Brugel and Van Gogh. My passion for exploring the city had ignited me to have a visit to the other hostel-Brugel, where some of my friends were staying, which was a few miles away. Brussels is one of Europe's must-see destinations with its small-town charm, trendy bars and restaurants, with fabulous food and sizzling nightlife. Fantastic shopping options, numerous museums, exhibitions and festivals add attraction to this diversified town.

Nightlife in Europe had always been a prime reason to keep youngsters like us out of hostel the entire night. It was truly said that half the country is awake at night to experience the charm of the city.

Like all, I too decided to explore the night life. I walked to the hostel where other friends of mine were staying. I was overwhelmed with constant thoughts of fulfilling my dream. From childhood, it was a dream to receive education from abroad, explore the world, meet new people and experience the culture of different countries. I was grateful for the moments when I wandered on the streets of Europe.

I landed up at a narrow street bound by ancient, structured mansions and bushy trees in between the walls. A long, straight street, ended up with a 5-storied building. It was the hostel – Brugel. The open windows with visible shadows from inside on the upper floors of the hostel showed that the other friends were still awake. Brugel was grounded with a large open space downstairs, with a food court outlet, and a few seats for dining. Some of my friends were there, and I got to spend some valuable time with them. It was midnight, a usual chilled out dark foggy climate. A bonfire setup by the hostel attendant was an added feature to our gossip session. Around mid-time some other friends joined us too. Food, drinks and topics related to some business start-ups were our topics of discussion. Time passed by and I realized that it was half past one and I had to return back to my hostel – Van Gogh which was just 30 mins by foot.

I decided to walk back to my hostel after bidding goodnight to my friends. On my way back to the hostel, I thought why not take the other street, so as to explore something different. Once again, the passion to explore something new, inspired me to go take the other route. I took the other street and after a while, I was trying to locate my street to connect it withthe original street I had taken in the evening, I realized that I had lost my way. Nowhere did the street look similar, neither the architecture. In such a situation – a new city, unknown streets, dark night, being alone, created fear and frustration in my mind. I thought it would be better to seek some guidance to find my way, but there was not a soul in sight. No one was there – only closed shops, lighted buildings and dispersed trees, which seemed to be the only living beings across my eye curvature. Being helpless, I turned left and went ahead to find a suitable place to sit, till I could find anyone to ask for directions. I swept the rectangular pavement, in front of a closed shop. I sat down there with my jackets and caps on with a high hope to see someone soon.

My hopeless expectation turned fruitful, when I saw someone

coming my way.

She was a lady - tall, slim and fit, wearing a fitting dress. As she moved towards me, I gazed at her looking for some help. I was lost in her beauty and curves, as she was just about to pass me. I hesitated to ask her for help to get me out of this situation at the earliest.

"Pardon me! – but I need your help" – I requested her. She turned around and looked at me. I was afraid and at the same time ardent to talk to her.

"Yes!" - she replied.

"I'm new to this city and have lost my way". Could you please help me find the street towards Van Gogh?" I asked

"Van Gogh?" She replied with confusion.

"Yes! Van Gough, near Sebastian Street." I clarified it.

Oh! Yes – that comes in my route. You can join me; I'm going through the same way." She answered.

I followed her, she was heading towards the nearby tram station, and so was my direction. I was expecting that she would talk to me, ask about me, where I was from and so on. But no! She was busy listening to music with round grayish cans attached.

We reached towards the tram station. Within a minute, the last tram for the day arrived. Except a handful of people, the tram was empty. The lady sat next to me with no expression, no discussion. She was probably in her early 20s and was dressed as if on her way back from a party.

I thought that she would inform me about my station. But no! She was busy with her music. The tram stopped at a station and she gave me a sign to get down there. Both of us went out of the tram and I realized it was the last station perhaps. I flew with the motion of her assistance. She gave me a signto go towards right and she went away straight towards a bushy dark street. I was amazed with her activity. I was fooled. My current situation was worse than before. I was far away from my destination. I concluded that probably the girl was drunk and not in her senses.

I assured myself "Everything happens for a reason". Anything odd happening, stretches a good incident. I was repetitively getting the intuition of something positive happening. Being hopeless and directionless I headed towards a square. "I think I should spend the night here, till the tram service starts" – I convinced myself. After that I didn't expected anyone's help, just waited for the sun to rise. I landed up at a symmetrical square – surrounded by mansions and palaces. The square was constructed in a typical Viennese new – classical style which attracted me a lot. In the heart of the square stood the equestrian statue of Godefroid de Bouilon, the legendary crusader and king of Jerusalem. Diagonally right to the statue ahead, there was a church. I headed towards it, planning to spend the night there, till the tram started.

Attached to the entrance of the church there was a big hall – it seemed like a pilgrim's rest place. Outside the hall was a big verandah, extending towards the entrance of the hall. I sat there cozily holding my jacket.As the night passed,, the temperature fell drastically. Shivering, I waited for the tram service to start. With various thoughts, extreme tiredness and the chilling weather, I closed my eyes. I slept there facing the wall of the hall. I was in deep sleep, when the church bell rang. In the early morning as I woke, I checked the time; it was 4 o'clock in morning. I felt like sleeping for some more time, as it was still dark but my eyes focused on a gathering inside the hall through the window, which was just above my head.

It was a less dense gathering of not more than 30 people. One strange thing was, that all of them seem to be in their late 40s. A major fraction of the crowd seemed to be professors, scientists or most probably researchers. They had dense white hair and were layered with long coats. "Itmight be a pilgrim group from other countries and are resting here" – I thought and decided to go back to sleep again but my ears captured the words like "thoughts, beliefs and dreams". I woke up and sat down. These people are talking about some topics of my interests. My eyes opened, ears got doubly activated to understand the content of their discussion.

I understood that at least these people were not on pilgrimage, but some highly qualified researchers from the local city, and were having some discussions. I tried to hear their words; mostly the major concentration was on the speaker's words. Only one person was speaking and the rest were listening to him. They surrounded him with notepads on their laps.

The speaker was a priest – probably the 'pastor of the church'

– with full white robe covering his entire body. My attention was focusedon his words. I was listening to him.

"It's a power that can give you everything – happiness, health

and wealth.

Whatever you want to achieve - you can, whatever you want to be – you can become,

No matter how big it is – the type of house you want to live in, the business you want to have, the relation you desire."

He was speaking about some power and his words were tilted towards spiritualism. The subject was interesting. It said that by knowing this power, probably I can achieve everything that I can

– this fascinated me. I wanted to know more about it. I wanted to enter the hall and join the rest of the audience but I was scared thinking, what if those people would kick me out for being an unknown outsider.

"I have seen magic happening in many people's life – financially, physically and spiritually too. It's everything that was possible because some people understood the "magic of thoughts" and have used these thoughts effectively." – *Father explained in a humble voice.*

With the increase in hesitation, my interest too increased. I slowly entered the hall with uncertainty. I was afraid of humiliation, but NO! The father welcomed me and offered a seat.

Sit down my son – he signaled me to take a seat.

I took a place in the middle of the circumference of the circlemade by them. I was feeling uncomfortable in the gathering of aged people and many of them not having any notepad to write. I was quite sure that I would learn more even without the notes.

What's that magic he was talking about, by which we can achieve everything? What is that concept which my parents have never shared with me, neither my teachers nor professors- I questioned myself.

Knowingly or unknowingly people use this power. Let me explain what I know about it – *he continued.*

"I was curious, my attention was only towards understanding the meaning of the power which can give me everything- a car I want, the higher qualification, my past relationship, name, fame and what not" – *I was excited.*

Every one of us is guided by this one universe, under a single power which controls everything of the universe – it's a power of the universe – that's attraction - he continued.

The universe follows the law known as law of attraction. It's the law which is identical throughout the universe. It doesn't matter which part of the world you belong to. It's applicable everywhere, every time and to everybody. The concept saysthat everything that comes into your life, you are attracting it to your life. All those things get attracted by the thoughts and the images that you hold in your mind".

"How can my thoughts attract everything? I questioned myself in the gathering. Everybody was noting down the points, the priest shared. But I was in a big confusion about the topic. I decided to question him to clear my points. I will never meet these people again to share such wonderful and magical concepts." – I thought but at the same time my ears were receiving all his words. Everything that's going on in your mind, you are attracting it into your life – he stressed.

Why is it that only some people of the world have everything and others can't – because these people have understood something which is the biggest asset of our life – it's our thoughts. Understanding our thoughts, knowing how thoughts can change our life, applying and having control over our thoughts can give us everything we want in our life.

Attraction! thoughts, and its applications, these were quite confusing for me. This time I decided to ask questions. I wanted clarity on these concepts – I decided.

But "attraction" – how? – I asked him. How can I attract everything I want?

That means, everything that happened till now in my life is what I attracted – my studies, my health, and my lifestyle?

Everything was attracted by me? I was shocked. "Yes, my son – you have attracted" – *he answered.*

"As a human being it's our duty to understand and think about the things that we really want," *he added and continued.*

We should be very clear in our mind about what we really want – a crystal-clear picture in mind. This is where you start getting into the principle of attraction or the magic of thoughts.

"Having a clear mind" is the first step to start using the power of thought

It's because what you think about, you become that – it gets attracted. Thus, the basic of the thought is "Thoughts get materialized".

The concept was new. Everything that we think about, it comes towards us and gets attracted magnetically. I was able to relate these concepts to my life too. I had always thought of pursuing higher education, study abroad, luxurious life, a famous personality and many more. I was able to connect that I had too, materialized a lot, the thought I used to have from my childhood – a higher degree, pursue studies abroad, early age business, a fan following, a wonderful house, good and positive friends."

"I slipped into these thought as I looked at the priest – who was still trying to make his topic more interesting and deeper."

Many people don't understand their thoughts – *he added and Continued.*

Our thoughts too have some frequency. We can measure our thoughts. Any thought that you trigger repetitively, it creates an image in your mind. You want to live in a wonderful house, want to have a luxury car, own your business, a perfect relationship etc. When you create such images, you send these signals in the sense of a frequency to the universe. Now remember that the thoughts are magnetic in nature and have their own frequency. When you keep thinking, the thoughts in the wave of frequency are sent to the universe, they magnetically attract similar things on the same frequency. Everything that is attracted is sent back to the emitted source and the emitted source is you.

I was overwhelmed with the information he shared. Now I am able to understand that, "as we think, so we become". It's we who design our future in our present thoughts. By the time I was trying to connect my past thoughts to my present life, a gentleman from the crowd raised his voice.

Father! - The gentleman called.

(Father looked to his left side, towards the gentleman)

"If the power of thoughts, principle of attraction is for all, and it exists everywhere, then why are many people unhappy? Why are the poor, poorer? Why are all people unable to live the life they want? Why are their dreams not fulfilled?"

He bombarded the priest with questions and it was quite valid at the time.

I understand it – my son! *(Father replied).* This is the most common question I usually address all fellow beings with.

The problem is not in the universe or the power of universe or attraction. It's not the universe that makes you unhappy or poor. The problem is within people. Most people think about what they don't want, rather than what they want. They just wonder why the same negative things happen to them. The reason why people don't have all the things they want are because they constantly think about the thing they don't want and expect to get the thing they want. The universe doesn't response to the thing that you want or don't want – it responds to the process of your thoughts and the images you hold in your mind. When you hold on to the image you want, you remain on a positive frequency and the universe creates the situation, gives you the people, attracts circumstances for you to get the thing you held in your mind. Once you understand the situation, people and the circumstance created by the universe, the next step is to take action.

The lines connected quite well to my current situation. I lost my way to the hostel, the initiative by the girl to help me, me landing up at the church square and now I was attending this orientation, everything happened automatically. Circumstances were created, people met and I landed up gathering the knowledge that I always wanted to know. For a long time, I always wanted to know the real meaning of our existence and the power of our human thoughts. This was the introduction.

I was lost in my thoughts trying to connect my life with the knowledge that I was receiving, but at the same time the father's words were occupying the spaceof my mind.

When you focus on the thing that you don't want, your mind creates an image accordingly (He stressed with a special expression). If you think you don't want to be late because of traffic, your mind creates an image of traffic jam. You attract the same in your life and you will be caught in the traffic and you will be late. The power of universe or the law works constantly, it responds to your thoughts every time. You cannot stop it.

The law of attraction is the law of creation. It works with the flow of thoughts and is a continuous process. Whatever you do at a particular point in time, your mind is working, whether you talk to somebody, listen to someone, watch a movie, think of your past, present or future, the flow of thoughts continues.

Focusing on what you want is very important. Controlling your thought is an inherent skill in human beings. Thousands of thoughts come every day but being human we should maintain and hold on to the thought we want. This consistent thought is the dominant thought which turns fruitful. Scientists, quantum physicists, researchers etc., different people gave different name to this concept. But I call this the "Magic of thoughts' – or a fruitful thought.

– He stressed on it.

Thousands of thoughts come every day. How to understand which thought is negative or positive? How to hold on to the thought we want? I interrupted him and asked in confusion.

"Yes! You can know your thoughts by your feelings."

He answered and continued.

"You can know what you are thinking by observing your feelings. The feelings let us know, what we are thinking and what we attract. It is impossible to feel bad while having good thoughts. Bad thoughts give bad feelings; good thoughts create good feelings. Your feelings determine the thoughts you have, tell us the frequency at which we exist at the time."

"It's feelings!" *I was bewildered.*

"Yes! My son, its feelings" *He said and continued.*

Certain positive feelings such as love, gratitude, passion, excitement, satisfaction, joy, hope, enthusiasm, etc. create a positive frequency and attract positive incidents, people, circumstances and events to your life. Whereas certain negative feelings such as irritation, hatred, anger, envy, disappointment, guilt, etc. create a negative frequency and attract negativity to our life. Once the bad feeling is experienced, you must understand that you are on a bad frequency. It implies that this is the time to change the frequency to the good ones.

Just remember some of the happiest memories of your life or listen to your favorite songs, go for a ride, etc.

The highest frequency you can emit is from the feeling of love. Love for anything good you want. The best dress you have, the food you love, the book you love the most, the relation you adore from the heart, or may be anything. The feeling of love is the strongest feeling.

"Feelings are fine! *(I added)*, but it's very difficult to be on the positive frequency always, in this society filled with negative vibes. How can we be on the side of positive feelings?" – I asked.

This time I felt as if he may get irritated with my continuous questioning. But no! He was quite passionate to tell us everything in a way we can understand.

Gratifications! *(He answered)*

"The best way to be on the frequency of good feeling is by the process of gratitude. Being grateful to all the things that you have can give you a good feeling. This keeps you on a positive frequency. You can list down all the things and the activities for which you are grateful. A pen you are holding, the blue shirt you have, the relation you are into, the money you have, the good memories you hold with your partner, the award you got, family members, or anything for which you are grateful. Just list down all the points to be grateful and say "Thank you" to each and every thing. Being grateful for something creates a positive feeling within us. This creates a feeling of happiness and joy and attracts happiness to your life."

"Many people remain in the sea of scarcity because they are never grateful for what they have. Most people always think that, I don't have the house that I want; I don't have the car that I want, I don't have the money I want, I don't have the partner I wanted. I don't have this; I don't have that. They always remain on the frequency of not having the things that they want and they remain on the same frequency till they change their thoughts from don't want to what they want. Think of what you want and be grateful for the things that you already have. The universe will give you those things more and more for the things you are grateful for."

It was a wonderful experience, feelings were empowered, I was grateful to the priest I was thanking the universe for losing my way to hostel, the girl helping me land here and the priest sharing wonderful information.

"Attraction, thoughts, feelings, and gratification" – it's wonderful knowledge you shared. I thank you heartily for sharing this.

– I thanked.

"Father! These concepts are very deep. What one thing we should follow to be in the process of this attraction - which can connect all these concepts" *I asked and decided it wouldbe the last question from my side.*

"Smart!" Father replied.

"It's a smart question." he smiled.

"The most fun and valuable experience that I could ever describe is the game of visualization. Seeing it, feeling it, exploring it, being with my dream, visualizing it, is the funniest thing that I practiced in every part of my life that I would advise everyone to do." *He stressed with a demanding voice.*

"Visualization has never-ending importance in our life because; imagination is something that can be created in your mind only and the mind is something that can create anything you want. There is no bar and selection to the power of visualization."

It seems he had dived into his personal life to describe the concept.

Visualization is simply a powerful thought in the form of images in your mind and a good feeling for the things you want. It creates a thought and the feelings of having those things in your life. When you visualize something, it creates a picture in your mind and it emits a powerful frequency to the universe. As per the law of attraction, the universe keeps hold of same and returns it to you exactly the way you hold it in your mind.

Yeah that's right – *I conveyed to myself.* At this point of time I was able to recall one of my friend's experience. A friend of mine had told me several times about the car he wanted. He dreamt of Fiat Linea. He was completely in love with the brand. He pasted the pictures wherever he could see them – all over his room, in front of his bed, as wallpaper on his phone, desktop background and felt as though he already possessed the car. He was consistent withthese thoughts and had visualized it as top priority. The miracle happened two years later.

He was only 22 years old then, the youngest in the locality to possess a Fiat Linea.

The beauty of the visualization was that, he got the same car, same model and the color he had visualized, that too at a discounted price. A week after he bought his car, the price went up. – I was trying to connect his experience with the concept described.

Visualization is an effortless process to get connected with what you want – father stressed.

Time passed. I was immersed inthese concepts, connecting my past life with the present one, visualizing the process I learnt from father. The concepts were so deep for me that I was not at all aware that it was morning outside. I looked back at the hall entrance and its daylight outside. Suddenly my mind took a transition from "attraction" to "tram". I decided to come back from there; else I might not catch the early morning tram to reach my desired street.

I stood up, thanked father for the wonderful lesson and came back from there. I walked towards the tram station. Boarded there and sat down with my thoughts. I was feeling that everything was happening automatically – starting from "losing my way" to "getting this tram" to my hostel. I was so happy that I felt as if I was filled with knowledge. This knowledge was wealthier than the management studies for which I was in Europe. I was able to feel the transition in my mindset and thoughts. My mind was filled with attraction, frequency, images, feelings and visualizations rather than branding, marketing and strategies.

From that day, this topic became my top priority among all the management books. Universe, quantum physics, feelings and visualizations became one of my favorite subjects of research after strategy and business innovation. After that I started finding out people, organizations, personalities who knew more about these concepts and of course books too. I started attracting people, circumstances and dignitaries who knew more about it. I came across trainers, communities, societies who taught me a lot about similar concepts.

An intentional thought will align your activities to meet like-minded people and to help them in their path of success– thus it's a "fruitful thought". The power of your feelings, love and gratifications will always be a source to make others successful and that starts from your intention to be successful. There's a demand for you to be successful, to attract people who want to be successful.

Summary

- *The power of the universe is something that can give you everything that you want in your life.*
- *Law of attraction states that "Whatever comes into your life is what you attract to it".*
- *Your present is the future of your past.*
- *You are the one who welcomes the universe to come into play.*
- *The universe responds to the thoughts and the image you hold in your mind.*
- *The dominant thought is the thought that creates your life and that is why it is a fruitful thought.*
- *The thoughts you hold in your mind are attracting like things to your life with similar frequency.*
- *Focus on what you want, rather than what you don't want.*
- *Be completely clear about your "real want" and have a constant focus to attract that into your life.*
- *Universe responds to the feelings you are having. A positive feeling such as love, passion, gratitude etc. creates positive frequency and attracts positive things in your life. Negative feeling attracts negative frequency.*
- *The best way to be on the frequency and good feeling is through the process of gratitude.*
- *When you visualize something, it creates a picture in your mind. It creates a thought and the feelings of having those things in your life.*

A fruitful Thought: Self-answered section

- Write down two activities which should be your major focus for the next three months.
- Describe the step-by-step procedure for the next three months to stick to your focus point.
- List down ten activities that make you feel good.
- List all the achievements and activities for which you are grateful.

4

Journey of Belief System

"Follow your bliss and the universes will open doors for you where there were only walls".

- Joseph Campbell

Every morning we wake up with a reason to fight for success. The reason may be anything, but at the end of the day everyone expects success and victory. What does success mean to you? There are various reasons for being successful. Success means personal victory, getting what you want, fulfillment of a personal need, a personal relationship, bank balance, a good lifestyle. Success means giving your best in your chosen field. It means being a man of name and fame. Success means leading. Success means happiness and living life to the fullest – the achievement of your goals. Success means having social recognition - achieving what others expect from you. Success means living your passion. Success is all about achieving what you always wanted. Success means having "The real want" in your hand.

Success means having "The Real Want" in your hand

During my Sales career days, I heard a lot of negative feedback from my associates. They said that they worked day and night, approached prospects on a regular basis, and did their work according to the training given, but everything was in vain as there was no positive outcome. I noticed the same thing with my college and university friends too. They studied hard, tried to start their own business, wanted to build relationships, find recognition in the college, but never succeeded. It was a big question for me – what's the problem behind it? When every effort is going in the positive direction, then what's making things collapse? I thought deeply about the issue, analyzing it from every angle and arrived at a very simple reason behind this feeling of nothingness.

Each one of us needs success. Everybody wants to reach the top, wants to win, achieve fame, and become famous. Nobody wants to be a subordinate and work under somebody– everybody wants to be independent. It doesn't happen with everyone, when people work hard but with no belief in themselves – they end up being unsuccessful. Being successful or not, the major factor depends on the pattern of our belief system – the power that changes one's world. The choice always depends on an individual. Believing in yourself helps create power within you, developing an attitude to do the work which can really change the results of the efforts you bring to your work. A strong belief generates the power, skill and energy to do the work you want and helps achieving it.

Let me share one of my experiences, in this context. Before starting my professional life, I was not exposed to the reality of business and sales, and I had experienced a lot of ups and downs at my work. Every day was a subtle day for me. Initially I was not able to sell my products. My products were sold after presenting to hundreds of prospects before which it was a failure all along. It shook my confidence and I became frustrated with the "attitude to fail" every time. When I reached the bottom of my expectations I analyzed myself, my attitude and my action plans and realized that I was missing the most basic yet the most important ingredient of success, i.e. belief. It was sometime in the month of December- the chilly winter, and Christmas knocking at the door. I still remember the vibrant evening which gave me a fine introduction to the basics of belief system. The event created a rhythm of belief– a simple event but made a mark on my inner sense of understanding.

The evening recorded the biggest ever youth leadership summit in our locality. When I reached the venue, I could see it was bursting with youth – thousands of youngsters belonging to the student community. Everyone stood by staring at the long red carpet pavement for the speaker's entry. Approximately five minutes later the speaker approached the stage and started his speech. A business tycoon, self-made millionaire, with a fan-following of thousands across the nation - started the speech with his introduction followed by a recent incident.

He started, "Last morning, when I was in Delhi, I was addressing some thousands of youngsters. I was busy solving their queries and I never realized I was running out of time, although the train was scheduled after 30 minutes. The ride from the venue to station would generally take around one hour. I somehow wound up the event and ran for the train. I was already late – the departure time had crossed and I was still on my way to the station. The driver kept on saying that I would miss the train but I assured myself that nothing negative would happen. I whole heartedly believed the train would be at the station when I would reach. I quite strongly believed that the train would be at the station. I could visualize the train waiting for me on the platform, all the way while travelling to the station. It took me around one hour to reach and I was happy to see that the train was still there, he said. It left after he entered it. He described this incident as the result of 'Power of belief'."

At that time when I heard him, I was not able to believe him. I never knew what it was – a miracle, was an accident, just a coincidence, or it was a luck, but it happened? I had heard about similar incidents many times and from other sources also. That day inspired me to learn more about the power of belief system. I recalled the famous saying that "Belief can even move mountains". I was not able to believe, until I realized the power of belief.

When I tried to relate this concept with my failure in sales career, I could find out that, I had no belief in myself, or in the product I was trying to sell. I never believed that I could win and taste success. The moment I felt the power of belief, my thoughts took a fine look at each and every activity of mine. It boosted my morale and gave me confidence to achieve what I want in any sphere of life.

The job of a person is to maintain his JOBS:

Since the days of my intermediate classes I came across the word job. Studying hard for a job, doing a job, earning a good salary and having a good decent life were the goals we had to achieve. From my parent to teachers and well-wishers, everybody taught me to work hard for a decent job. People believe that working day and night for a company can give them good life, but they don't realize that to perform well in their job they need to go through their JOBS.

On the very 1st day of my engineering college we were programmed to understand the basic and the main objective of our education was to get us a good job as it would help us accomplish our dreams. The lessons repeated themselves when I enrolled for my management degree. Everyone directed us to focus on only one thing; job. I didn't know how a job could help fulfill my dreams – reach my destination, give me a life of abundance but I surely was blessed to learn something from the word JOB, which helped in my spiritual growth.

Everybody advised me to work hard and get a decent job. However, no one taught me how to achieve it. Schools and colleges invest a huge amount in training students, improving their soft skills, analytical skills, etc. and prepare them for a good job, but they miss out on developing the inner power and strength of a student. The inner power is something that can give a human being everything he wants; it is our inner belief system. A belief system strengthens our inner will and purifies the thought process – which helps in building a good thought and it is that good thought which creates our own future. I strongly believe that we are responsible for anything good or bad happening in our life and this is strongly connected to our own belief system.

For me, the meaning of the word job is "Just Obey your Boss", but I came across another meaning i.e. Journey of belief system (JOBS). The main job of a person is to maintain JOBS. We need to pass through the journey of our belief system, our JOBS – the factor that will help us achieve our "Real Want". Let us divide this journey into three categories:

- Belief in the system
- Belief in the work
- Belief in yourself

Belief in the system:

Belief plays a big role in each and every dimension of your life. It is very important to have faith in the system in which you are involved. It may be your college, your company, or your home. I lacked belief in the company where I worked. What could the company do for my life? Why care for something that is not my own, I thought. The reality is that the system you are serving is the system which is paying you in terms of happiness, money and satisfaction. In return, the system also expects something from you and belief in the system is what we can give.

Many of my friends took admission in college without the belief that a college can change their life, though in reality they should have considered college as one that would build their career. A person who believes that the system is wrong will find the system going wrong for him and will be unsuccessful. However, the one who sees the positive aspect and believes in it will definitely achieve success within the system.

The belief in the system will generate a power to act on your plan – a power to act, implement and perform follows belief in the system. Belief forms a continuous thought which can be positive.

Belief in the work you do:

I have heard many people say how they hate the work they do, how they are compelled to do it for the sake of money, how the repetitive nature of their work frustrates them. On the other hand, there are people who keep doing their work till they complete it. They complete their primary work before accepting any secondary activity. They return home content after the completion of their day's work.

In which category of people do you belong? The first type of people are always in a state of frustration. They get tense; they are completely bored and feel as if they are working under a lot of pressure. The same happens with some of my friends. Sometimes they behave as if they are about to commit suicide for the work pressure and their incapability to complete the work. The second category of people are always in a state of happiness. They don't lose focus and concentrate on their work. The above categories have the same workload but one succeeds while the other doesn't.

The major difference is not in the work, individual potential or situation but the magnitude of love and belief a person has for the work.

When one believes in the work he does, it creates a positive tune for the work – a sense of ownership, passion for the work, love for the work, inner satisfaction and a reason to complete the work with success. Most people find it hard to believe in their work from the heart because they do the work forcefully. When, the reason for doing the work changes from compulsion to "love for work" individual success is achieved.

"Do the work because you love to work,
not because you have to do it"

Belief in yourself:

You can believe in the work you are doing, or the system you are in, only if you have complete belief in yourself. If you don't believe in yourself then the direction you are headed for is not going to help you achieve your 'Real Want'. Being aware of that direction is always an advantage; else the results will not be favorable. There will be confusion and the situation will become critical rather than productive. The factor that brings everything on track is a strong belief system. As truly the adage goes, "Belief can move mountains".

During the induction stage of our management course, the college had organized a drama competition, within the different branches. Students were selected from top universities with highest grades and were invited from almost all parts of the country. The environment of camaraderie had still not developed among us, so our coordination was nil within our class mates. We were given a few weeks to prepare the Shakespearian play – Macbeth. Due to ego clashes, communication gaps, and mismanagement we ended up wasting time and lost around ten effective days without any valuable preparation for the play that we would have to present in front of the college, faculty, management executives and chief guests.

With just four days to go, one of our competitors came to our class and invited us to attend their play on the day of competition.

We were not at all prepared for the play. It was shocking for our entire class and made us feel ashamed and guilty for the disunity we had shown. We were new to the college, our faculty's reputation, batch's reputation, our potential and credibility were at stake. The result of the competition would define the potential of our batch mates.

We had only three days left; we started the preparation with a mind not to win but just to participate but I was focused on the fact that if we are participating then we must participate to win, else our efforts would be meaningless. I was completely sure about this one challenge. We started working hard as a team. We all motivated each other for an intense preparation. Soon we were ready with our play, script, backdrop, costume, make-up etc. Though everything was not perfect we worked as a team. There was a lot of negativity and opposition from some of the members, but I had complete faith that we would win.

Having disbelief is also a kind of power. When you disbelieve anything, your mind attracts the reasons and circumstances to have doubts about your results. I was very sure about the results even before they were declared. When we won, nobody was willing to believe it. We were able to create everything out of nothing. It was a time of glory for all of us, as it was the first victory of our batch as a team.

Why did I share this experience? It is important to know that each and every situation and incident that happens in life or is about to happen is due to somebody's belief. Believing in the result that you want is a strong driving force, a power. Belief in the ability to be successful is a background of every successful man. Belief in yourself and the work you are doing can not only move mountains but do more than that. A strong belief can change the situation. Once a person believes in something, he can easily achieve it. If he believes that he can handle a big task, act accordingly and achieve it. You can become a giant in your field, and the factor which helps is the 'belief in yourself'.

"The Believe World"

Once you start loving your job, your situation and your circumstances, and most importantly you...will set forth on the road to achieving your "Real Want". Many times, it happens that people do not love themselves. They see themselves in the mirror and say, "I'm not handsome, I can't do the task, and I'm not going to be successful because I'm not a person of potential. They blame themselves, their failures, and their weakness. By doing this they lose faith in the future. One should think the other way. If you stand in front of the mirror and say; I'm very handsome, I'm great, I'm going to be successful, I can do it; and then a self-belief will be activated. Once this is done a fire starts in your heart to achieve your 'Real want" - The more the fire burns within you, the higher you will reach.

A person's result is due to his thoughts and the thought you have can be changed and managed by the love you have for your work and especially the love for yourself. Such feelings create a strong belief that in turn leads to positive thoughts. The thought you have will manifest itself leading to positive results. Having belief and managing thought positively and programming your mind for success is something that can create a right direction to achieve "The real want".

"Exercise and program your mind to achieve your "Real Want"

Think about what you want; don't focus on what you don't need. Think about your success, not about your failure. When you are in a problem think about your solution, don't think how to give up. While facing the challenges, think that you can win because you have the potential to do so. Think "I can do it". Create a habit to "do it now" and not tomorrow. Not thinking about your success is similar to planning for your failure. Be more focused and have belief in your work and your "Real want". Extraordinary people are not extraordinary due to their extraordinary work, but because of an ordinary, continuous conviction in their work.

"Not thinking about your success is like planning for your failure"

Equation of success:

When you visualize a crystal clear "REAL WANT" with the complete belief in your ability and willingness to achieve it and act with the fire of burning desire in the correct direction, success always follows. The success is the achievement of the "Real Want"

Vision + belief + burning desire + challenging work = Success.

It's not "how" people become successful but it's the power of their belief which channelizes them for success. It's the reason to remember that "to be successful", you have to go through your JOBS. The importance of your words, the values of your ideas and your existence should make an impact in society. People should believe you, and for that you have to be labeled as a successful personality, in turn to achieve that, you should believe the work you are doing, the system you are associated with and most importantly a strong "Belief" in yourself.

Summary

- Success means having "The Real Want" in your hand.
- People really work hard, but they don't achieve everything they want because they don't ever believe that they can achieve it.
- A strong belief generates the power, skill and energy to do all the work you want and helps in achieving it.
- The crucial job of a person is to maintain his JOBS.
- "JOBS" is a journey of our belief system - belief in the system, the work you are doing, and in you.
- The more you believe in your system, the more you will succeed.
- The most important thing is the magnitude of love you have for the work you do.
- Do the work because you "love to do it", not because you "have to do it".
- You can believe your system and the work you are doing, if you completely believe in yourself.
- Having disbelief is also a power.
- The more fire you burn inside; the greater heights of success you reach.
- Not thinking about your success, is like planning for your failure.

Journey of Belief System: Self-answered

Section A:

- *Write down three positive points about the system within which you work.*
- *Write down two points about your system, which differentiates your system from others. Analyze and describe clearly, how this above point will help you achieve your "Real Want".*

Section B:

- *Write down all the activities you are doing in your profession and have a clear idea about them.*
- *From the above list, select the activity you love the most and write down why you love it.*
- *Write down how the activity you love will help in achieving your "Real Want".*

Section C:

- *List down all the qualities you have, for which people like you.*
- *Describe with feelings how you are going to use that quality to achieve your "Real want".*

5

A Meaningful Attitude

"When everything seems to be going against you, remember that the airplane takes off against the wind, not with it."
- Henry Ford

Certain incidents, learning curves, pleasing environments always remain in our mind. Have you ever experienced or met any personality who has pleased you to some extent?

Have you ever met any person who created a vibration of energy in you? Have you ever met any person whose words inspired you or people whose thoughts impressed you so much that you aspired to be like him/her?

It happens with everybody. I'm talking about people who leave an unforgettable impact on you from the very first meeting – whose presence creates a positive environment, inspires all, and gives a reason to go ahead. Such people are able to create a sensational wonder because of the "Positive attitude" they own.

Building your attitude:

Have you ever wondered why some people in your surroundings who are very successful, respected and easily noticed, intentionally they are given priority and are loved by the majority? It is not a hidden quality, potential or brilliance which made them exceptional and outstanding. It is their attitude. Attitude is something that defines the height of your success. The better the attitude, the more is your success – an attitude to act, react positively, selfless attitude to give, growing by changing and creating an attitude to inspire others are some areas which constitute a degree of benchmark. All people are not born successful. Every successful person has worked hard to earn it. These people have discovered themselves in the journey of success – they understood the effect of growth, learned the values of having a positive attitude and applied it to their own life – resulting in them reaching the level of success and creating a positive vibration.

A child at birth has no clue about "positive attitude. It is an attribute imbibed and developed from the environment it grows in. People learn from the people they meet, from the type of education they get; it is created and shaped by the external factors they resist and the internal factors that receive those teachings. The external factors may include friend circle, family, the surroundings, the education received, the incidents faced in everyday life, the work you do daily, the people you meet, the responses you give, and every occurrence in your life which counts in building your attitude. The internal factor is your conscience that receives those experiences and learning from your daily life. The most crucial factor, however, is you. You are the only person who undergoes the process of building your own attitude – the one who receives inputs from the environment and applies to the self.

An individual learns how to behave, how to react to others, how to act in a situation by observing the people in their surroundings - It may be your home, your workplace, your educational background, the cultural environment you belong to. At the end, it is all about the environment you live in. Creating, changing, sustaining the environment is all about the power of positive attitude. Environment is something that helps you in building your attitude - that leads to success.

Positive and negative attitudes in people are easily visible to others. People who are cool, calm, caring, respectful, confident and humble are positive and the attributes are easily noticeable. The quality they possess from within creates a positive vibration – their words, thought, decision, and action generates positivity. On the other hand, there are people who always remain upset without any specific reason; they blame the situations, circumstances and everyone they are living with. They are always dissatisfied with their friends, life partner, and work. Such people are pessimists who are negative about everything and find it difficult to be successful. Survival for these types of people in today's competitive world is very tough; this person creates a negative environment and stops other people's growth.

"Positive people create success; the negative ones destroy it"

Being positive is acceptable; it's exceptional and absolutely valuable, but it's not easy to change. To change ourselves from being negative to positive is very stressful and for some people it is even unimaginable. Some people love to be pessimistic, and promote negativity but at the end of the day these people fail drastically in their field. Their negativity becomes such an inherent part of their personality, that they are unable to accept any positivity. Since they don't admit their negatives, they don't change.

If you are having a favorable situation, your education is good, your environment is good, your learning experience is good, then you are definitely going to do good things. Your outcome will be positive. Think about it vice-versa, i.e., when your situation is bad, your experiences are bad, environment and education are poor, when you are in a situation of failure, there is no hope in your life, your situation leads you towards disappointment and leaves you disheartened. In such situations, your behavior and reaction to it will define your attitude. If you can survive in such unfavorable situation and continue to think positively then you are considered a person with positive attitude. Anyone can achieve success in favorable situations - when there is an unfavorable situation, people quit, they step back. The one who fights and thinks positively and comes out with a positive solution, stands out of the crowd and is always appreciated.

"Reacting positively even in a negative situation determines your positive attitude"

Attitude to act:

I have heard and read in many books that "Knowledge is powerful". Is knowledge truly powerful in today's competitive world? Today's technological sphere has made knowledge open for everyone. I have come across many people having prodigious knowledge, expertise in their field but are neither associated with success nor satisfied with life, not able to fulfill their wish, confused and disrupted in maintaining relationship, or are negative in social recognition and unable to lead and live their passion. They sit in the corner of their house expecting someone to come and appreciate them by patting their back.

Knowledge is powerful. It is the application of knowledge which makes it more powerful. Action on the set plans with proper utilization of knowledge creates success, inspires others, sets example and benchmarks, activates people to work hard, helps to achieve our "Real Want" and make us powerful, but having extraordinary knowledge and keeping it within us and not utilizing it is surely havoc at the end of the day. Paths open up when you step forward, not when you stand at one place waiting for the direction to be created.

There are people who think, analyze, and plan their workday dreaming without making any corrective action plan. This amounts to a loss of time and energy. Everybody agrees that thinking is important and making the right choice at the right time is equally important, but making an impact when the time has gone is of no use to the prior actions and analysis. Too much thinking is a waste of time. Applying the thoughts, acting and stepping ahead are footsteps towards manifesting the dreams. Either success or failure, but these footsteps constitute a concrete lesson for the learning curve. In order to successfully transform what is wrong to be right, one has to ACT.

"Stop analysis and start working, else someday analysis will lead to paralysis."

Attitude to change and grow:

Everyone who comes in our life, the situation we experience and every incident we face has some reason behind it. Each and every event that occurs in our lives comes with a lesson to be learnt. These episodes give us an opportunity to learn and embrace change if required. The crux is that, neither people grab these opportunities to learn and grow from them, nor do they change themselves for the better. We all are aware that "change is the only constant". Changing ourselves consistently as per the requirement of the situation keeps us on a track of continuous improvement. Every situation you face is distinctive and unique as compared to the previous ones. The culture you belong to may be different from your friends and fellow mates. Every pattern of your life gives you a reason to change and grow. Each and every human being you meet helps in your success provided you understand that and you are in a mindset to change yourself. It's very clear that:

"The moment you stop learning is the moment you stop growing"

Growing is the process of learning and letting knowledge enlighten us. Most people never accept their mistakes. They feel what they do is right, and consider everyone else wrong. They may be right, but it is not effective. Accepting their individual faults and adapting to change is necessary for personal development. Their feeling towards change is rigid. It is difficult to change a habit or an attitude, if you do not learn to change yourself with time. You should be prepared to face failure because "If you keep doing what you have been doing, you will keep getting what you have been getting." To achieve something new, to create a better environment, have better achievements, relationships, you have to be open to change and learn as much as possible. Changing oneself towards the direction to achieve the "real want" is obligatory.

"If you are not going to change yourself with time, then you are going to end up like dinosaurs in the past"

Selfless attitude and attitude to give:

The government constructs the road and charges us tax. The educational institutions charge us fees for educating us. We buy anything in exchange of money. We accept a relationship because we get love in return. Have you realized something? We give only with the hope to get something in return. Think about a tree that gives us fresh air, the sun which provides with light, nature and its components that give us free access to everything, without any expectation or return from us. This is what called a selfless attitude. They just follow the rules of the universe. But think, will human beings be able to do this? Will they develop a selfless nature and give for the sake of giving? If it happens, our surroundings will be glorious; everybody will start having a deep sense of humanity and then one day peace will reign across the globe. I would address the Sun as the biggest element of selfless attitude which shines the brightest, and so we can shine like it.

There are people who help because they hope to get something in return. They help, teach, and approach to gain something. If there is nothing in return and they stop helping people – ignore them, forget, and start avoiding. This will not make us shine. Help without having the expectation to receive, don't worry about the results. Give and you will receive much more than what you have given.

The attitude of being selfless – the "attitude to give" has created people's destiny. It has changed many lives across the universe, changed the direction of many people from failing to being extraordinarily successful. It's a universal power, universal law – "the more you give, the more you will receive". When you give from within, you create a positive feeling from your heart. That keeps you on a positive frequency, this is sent to the universe, and the universe, in return, gives you back the same thing magnified.

"The more you give, the more you receive"

A person can change his attitude. The process always starts from the "attitude to praise" or "attitude of gratitude". Start practicing to praise when you find something good. Be grateful for the life you have today, praise a person's behavior you like, any incident you like, anything you feel good in your life. This will create a positive energy within you leading to a positive attitude.

I have felt this power in my personal life. There was a time – I was not able to think positively, situations were bad, my life was not fruitful. I always tried to be a man of positive attitude but it was difficult to change. Transition in the thinking process was always a strong part of the learning curve. I started implementing the power of gratitude and praise – I started to praise my life, the activities I did, the food I ate, the road I travelled. For every moment thankfulness played a part in my thoughts. This resulted in changing my thinking process. It took some time but I completely recovered from some of the negative situations – it changed in such a way that I loved to promote positive values to others around me.

Attitude to react positively:

This experience travels back to the time when I was in the 4th standard. My alma mater was a convent that imparted strong values. As far as I can remember, it was first day of my class in standard 4th . Our class teacher told us a simple story that, in hindsight, taught me the value of reacting positively.

There was a farmer in a village. Every day he would travel to his farm miles away from his home. He was accompanied by his two sons, five and seven years respectively. The farmer used to work for the whole day till late evening, while both his sons used to play under the shade of a tree till they returned. This was their general routine. One day, tired and hungry from working under the scorching heat of the sun, the farmer called out to his elder son to bring lunch, he had forgot to bring. The elder son promised to get the lunch for him and disappeared. When he didn't return with the lunch for a long time, the farmer called out to his younger son for the same. The younger son asked him to get lunch for himself since he was busy playing. The boy was very young and the farmer did not expect much from him. However, the boy came back soon, handed the lunch over to his father and returned to his game.

Committing to do something and not doing it, and on the other hand taking actions without any expectations are different things. There are people who commit without respecting the promise. When commitment is not fulfilled it hurts, creates disturbances, breaks up relation, and makes the environment negative. The attitude to fulfill your commitment creates a positive environment

– it's all about building up the attitude to "do what you say".

Attitude to-do-it-anyhow:

Many people don't follow the course of action they need to follow. They get diverted by their friends, family members, roommates, and neighbors. They get influenced by others and pause in their action plans. This delays their success and leads to temporary frustration. A repetition of these activities can lead to the closing of the action plan. Kaput! End of the dream. A small mistake and failure in maintaining a proper attitude tends to a negative destiny.

Once the attitude to "do-it-now-anyhow" is developed, it is easy to handle such situations. I too have gone through such circumstances. Initially I used to pause my work and action plan and get distracted by friends and gradually do other work which was originally not a part of the action plan. I was unable to say "No" because I was worried it would ruin the relationship. When I realized that I was going out of my action plan I was forced to create an attitude "to do it anyhow". I used to plan the previous night and make my unavailability or inability clear to friends and acquaintances. Developing an attitude "to do it anyhow" and saying 'No" politely to useless activities is something that can minimize all obstructions. This increases your focus on the action plan and lead you to the direction of your "real want".

Avoid negative aspects in your life:

Life is full of positive and negative elements – it's a cycle and it happens on a regular basis. All environments cannot be positive. People vary from each other in culture, experiences and their mindset. The particular mindset of a person leads to creation of an environment around him. Life is uncertain – each and every situation you experience is imbued with positive and negative aspects. Positive only means 'positive'; it doesn't imply not being negative. Avoiding negatives and moving towards positive aspects – in terms of thought you carry, mindset you possess, people you keep company with, regular activity you do, food you eat, decision you take, do become strong reasons for your success path. A bad environment ignites an unwelcome negative thought – which attracts negative circumstances in your life making you more negative and prone to higher complicacy.

"To be positive it doesn't mean, not to be negative. Positive means positive only"

Think of a half-filled glass with black ink. If you want to fill it with white, you have to take out the black ink completely, wash the entire glass and then pour white ink in it. You cannot turn the half-filled black ink glass white by adding more and more white to it. The murkiness will persist. To retain the white color, you have to thoroughly wash the glass. In the same way being positive doesn't mean adding positives to your negative qualities, it calls for the elimination of all the negative qualities. The rest will be automatically positive.

Avoid indulging in conversations which can ruin relationships. In altercations, where relationship is at stake, I have found it best to ignore the words you don't like and concentrate on the words you like. Intelligently ignoring the negative qualities and accepting the positive will help in maintaining your learning curve and a good relationship. "Intelligent ignorance" removes the matter of disturbance, ego, misunderstanding and help in building up a positive ambience.

Attitude to get suggestion from right people:

The biggest mistake people commit is to take suggestion from a wrong person. Sometimes this could become the reason for one's failure. I spend the maximum time in my training session indeveloping and maintain a proper mindset among my associates. Generally, people get distracted from their path after having useless and senseless opinions from various people in different environments. It's very simple if you have a health problem, you will obviously consult a doctor, instead of your brother who is a great scientist. He may be a scientist, very knowledgeable and capable of sane advice, but he will not be able to cure you.

A very common incident occurs among colleges students. Students take admission in B-schools because they know that it will enhance their business skills and knowledge. After admission it has become a great trend among students to speak ill about the college, faculty and infrastructure. When the same thing happened in my college I happened to find out the root cause of these rumors and what I discovered was quite funny.

The B-school where I study is very good in terms of education, faculty, course and most other parameters to define a top B-school.

It has earned a big reputation in the past two decades. Many students took admission after evaluation because of its reputation and track record. After some days, those students who were very positive and happy about the school started spreading negative rumors based on what their seniors had told them. The new students based their allegations and criticism on what they had heard and lost all hope in the institution they had struggled to enter. Certain rumors regarding placements, faculty, infrastructure, etc. created problem for all other students. The seniors who had started those rumors are those with bad academic records throughout the entrance year, backlogs, and with no hope for placements. When suggestions were taken from brighter students, the answers which we got were contrary to what we'd heard. The hard working, sincere seniors said that the college was good along with the faculty and placements it offered - it is the personal effort which will make a difference.

It is the matter of environment with which we interact. A person owning and riding a motorcycle cannot be the right person to tell you the pros and cons of a particular luxury car; but a person who already owns a luxury car, knows more about it and can tell you what is involved in buying that luxury item – the hard work we need to put in, the direction we should put the efforts and the practical knowledge in achieving the same. It is good to take suggestion from our elders, family members, neighbors, friends and teachers and even from the internet, but we should be very sure that the source is a right one. An attitude or a habit of taking the right suggestion from a right person simplifies the effort to achieve the "Real Want".

Real want is an intention, where as a self-belief strengthens one's confidence and a proper attitude puts us in a right direction to implement. It's not about "how" a person becomes successful, but it's because of a firm practice with a meaningful attitude which makes them successful in achieving their "Real Want".

The society you belong to, the crowd who knows you, should understand the real value of the attitude you carry. A vibration of *"Meaningful attitude"* in you should attract more audiences. Everyone should accept you as an influential positive entity and for that you have to be stamped with the term "a successful one".

Summary

- People can create a positive environment because of the positive attitude they have.
- A person's attitude is created and shaped due of the external factors they resist and the internal factors that receive those teachings.
- A positive person creates success and the negative one destroys it
- People don't change because they don't accept their negativity.
- Your positive attitude will determine whether you can remain positive within a negative situation.
- Knowledge may be powerful, but application of knowledge is important.
- Excess of thinking is wastage of time that should be converted into action.
- The more you give, the more you receive – start praising.
- Develop a habit to "do-what –you-say" and practice to say "No" to unwanted things.
- Being positive doesn't mean not to be negative. Being positive means being positive only.
- Being positive doesn't mean adding more positives to your negatives qualities; it involves the removal of all the negative qualities.
- The habit of taking suggestions from the right person is important to maintain a constantly positive mindset.

A meaningful attitude: self-answered section

- Describe the environment you always like and want to focus on.
- List down the habits you want to change

- Write down all the activities, people, incidents for which you are thankful.
- Write down three activities which you want to put a habit to say "No" to it.

6

Invisible Leader

"If your action inspires others to dream more, learn more, do more and become more, you are a leader"

- John Quincy Adams

Realizing my leadership qualities, I conducted my activities with a different approach. I am neither a businessman nor a psychologist, neither a motivational speaker nor an orator, but simply a student. My cogitation went through a transition that changed my life and then surfaced a leader from within me. The difference was to apply my leadership qualities and crunch my potential to the highest level. I realized that leadership was not about just being the best but about doing extraordinary things out of nothing. I could smell the fragrance of success, the values of life, the importance of dreams in human life, and very importantly the desire to be a faithful human being first. My confidence increased and my vision became clear. I started reiterating the word "leader" in my mind and started leading in each and every situation for which I had the potential. With this realization, everything else fell in place.

Let me describe a portion of my background to depict the base of leadership. I come from a middle-class Indian family where my parents are not highly qualified – a family with basic ethics of simplicity, honesty and intimacy. My mother is an uncomplicated, helpful and a kind lady, my father is diligent, determined and simple. His immense struggle started from scratch by building values for family and so on has inspired me extremely. He started his career by earning a daily wage of rupees sixty somewhere in the mid of 1970's. Neither highly qualified, nor born to a wealthy father, his prime objective was to educate his children and give them the best facilities – a true scholastic and professional education, a decent lifestyle, a lovable family environment and what not. He was always focused on beinga genuine educator to us with richness of the education of life – the true lessons that life needs.

In the early 1980's my father was offered a position in the central government at a minimum salary. It was very difficult to manage a huge family with just a few hundred rupees for an entire month. Throughout my childhood, I rarely found him relaxing at home. He would return after I was asleep and would leave for work early morning even before I was awake. This was his daily routine. After investing nine extensive hours to the central government, he managed to start his own start-up firm for some extra income so as to provide a better life to his family. I had then realized that the reason for his effective workday and night was very simple - to achieve his "Real want". He had never got a chance to complete his education but always wanted to provide the best for his children, give them the best of both professional and real life education. Till date he has high expectations from all of us, which is natural. He was very confident about the results of the input he had given.

The day I left for Mumbai to pursue my management studies was a period of intense realization. I was waiting at the airport for the boarding call, when my father called me. His words made me a stronger person and helped me forget my past failures and begin a new life. I was expecting his suggestions, wishes and blessings to go ahead for my higher education, but it was more of a demand – to prove myself, be a leader in life and be the best with ultimate implementation of time, potential and capital. He said – "I have worked very hard, did my best to achieve what I am, today, and I hope that you too are going to do the same. Forget everything that has happened in your past and just focus on making yourself proud. This will be the biggest gift you can give me for my conscientious struggle."

His call got disconnected; it lasted for only few minutes. As I sat there, his words echoed in my mind again and again. My thoughts heaved across my potentials- giving me a strong reason to be the best with "what I have", to stretch myself to perfection, and prove myself to the peak of my ability. That was the moment when I promised myself, one day I would feature on the cover page of business magazines.

Throughout the journey, I thought about his struggle: from his initial days of earning sixty rupees per day to being the successful businessman he is now. The narration I shared here is not unique

– it's quite generic and familiar, but my learnings and observations somehow awakened the leader within me. I was able to realize his struggles with scarcity, rejections, sorrow and misery to feelings of abundant, wealth, fame and prosperity. His loyalty towards his "real want", and effectively implementing his action plan were quite different from the general society. A habit of practicing successful attitude – an attitude to plan, act and lead has always made a mark in my subconscious mind. An ability to take a long-term decision, while earning values, respect, and a heart for others was lauded by society. Giving priority to both personal and professional relationships equally, also shows a mark of true leadership quality.

My parents are the humblest couple I have ever known. They have everything because they have a big heart. They live a simple life and follow values with self-respect. What I have learnt from them and my past experiences have taught me a lot about human life and the purpose of living it. When I started writing about the lessons that I have learnt till today, I realized it had already turned into a book.

We always have an image of a leader as a famous person and we look up to him. We generally tend to follow and believe that only celebrities, famous industrialists, and politicians are our leaders. While penning down my thoughts, I realized that my leader was right beside me, moulding my life, giving me the right direction since the time I entered this world. I searched for my leader at every stage of life, every aspect of life, but my search ended when I found my leader was right within me. Most of us tend to go out in the world and explore the meaning of life and consider our external experiences as enlightening but we often miss out, not realizing the important role that our home, family and parents play in our lives to mould us. I strongly believe that a true leader must qualify to have these qualities:

L - Loyalty towards the Real want

E - Effective in implementing the action plans

A - Attitude to plan, act and lead

D - Decision maker

E - Earning values, respect and a heart for others

R - Relationship with everyone.

"A leader always lies within your family"

We just need to recognize them, understand and learn from them. My teachers taught me that "In order to be a successful person, you have to be a leader first". My mind often contravenes it. The most important question we need to ask ourselves is "Why do we have to 'be' a leader, aren't we all born a leader? Each and every one of us is born with some extra ordinary quality of a leader but we refuse to acknowledge the l-e-a-d-e-r within us. In order to do so, self-guidance, leading all circumstances, consciously taking decisions and implementing it are factors that will make all the difference.

Let us recall the small but real hardships that almost all of us have faced as adolescents. From, tying our shoelace to riding a bicycle for the first time were tasks that were very challenging to becoming accomplished at that particular age but as we grew up, we knew well how to perform the same with ease. Although, it was challenging then, but we kept trying until we succeeded. If we fell down while riding a cycle, we stood up and gave it a second try – we never gave up then. The most attractive part about the phase is about the attitude we possessed. We continuously struggled but never gave up until we succeeded. Adulthood is the magnified stage of our childhood phase, with added values, qualities and potential to our existence. If during adolescent, we could find the solutions through our struggle and efforts despite the challenge being arduous and new, I am very sure we have the qualities of a latent leader within us; all we need is to realize the right attitude and the hidden potential.

"A Leader exists in your family"

"Loyal"
Loyalty toward the Real W"ant

"Effective"
Effective implementations of plans

"Attitude"
Attitude to plan, act and Lead

"Decision"
Decision Maker

"Earning"
Values & Respect

"Relationship"
Understanding

As we grow up, our responsibilities, challenges and situations also propagate. We have to face new ultimatums at regular intervals; some of us cope up to face and scuffle to achieve personal victories, while some step back in the visage of the same objections. If we could find solutions and face challenges in our childhood without much knowledge and potential, why is it not possible for us to face challenges and succeed at this stage of our lives. As compared to our childhood; our challenges and responsibilities magnify with age and at this phase of life we have the understanding, the required knowledge and most importantly the available resources. What we all need to understand and utilize is the potential to accomplish what we desire and thus succeed as a true leader in our respective fields. Successfully accomplishing the duties and responsibilities in our respective lives is the sign of strong leadership. It is surely a confrontation, but how does one become a leader without facing challenges?

"Accomplishing the best in the field we are is all about being a strong leader"

A Leader requires no position to show true leadership:

A myth about being a leader is that only successful people who hold a high position or designation are considered as leaders. The truth lies in the very fact that a leader is one who does not require any position to lead, only the right determination to achieve his "real want" and give his best. The most important reason for sharing the story of my father relates to the same. He did not hold any position of a prestigious company nor was he wealthy; he was a man with the right purpose and had the qualities to set an example for me through his constant efforts. The most important lessons I learnt from him were, that a leader always sets an example and creates an environment for success and development for his followers. It made my purpose concrete and valuable. As quoted by Ross Perot;

"Inventory can be managed; people must be led by examples"

The moment we hear the word "Leader" we assume the person to be qualified and groomed for holding the highest rank, a famous politician, a successful businessman, or a wealthy knowledgeable activist. A leader doesn't require any position but it is the quality to take the "initiative to lead" and the "sense of responsibility" which makes an individual a good leader. A student can be a leader amongst his counterparts, leader may be found in an ordinary employee among other employees and the CEO in an organization. A person can only be a leader based on their ability to lead and achieve excellence in what he/she does – it is not about a position but about creating and setting examples. These examples inspire other, activate their conscience, enable strengths, show directions and create new success stories.

Successful people achieve what they aim for due to a clear vision – a prime factor which not only makes them successful but also grooms them to become true leaders. It's a sign of a true leader that makes them stand out of the crowd. Vision leads to right direction and this in turn leads us to work hard with devotion, thus converting a dream into reality through continuous implementation.

Leaders are created in demanding situations:

Our life is the most beautiful gift to us with various emotions

– happiness, sorrow, tragedy, the amazing feeling of love, and the destructive felling of hatred. We all go through these emotions and have a high and low phase in our lives. Like most of us, I too had a low phase in my life – with no hope for success, complete distraction, financial instability, illusions in relationships and what not. It took a lot of effort and I had to pass through a lot of struggle to achieve a name among the youth community. I conquered fame, success and popularity and the ability to dream big. I cherish the moment when I gave my first autograph to a young admirer. Although it gave me immense pleasure, but this was temporary. It was difficult for me to get back that same fame I had earned in society. My resignation had an adverse effect on my family and other relationships. It was a phase in my life where I had huge loss in business. My peace of mind was at stake and I ended up with several sleepless nights. My thoughts kept on attracting negativities I had always avoided

– distractions, dissatisfaction, failures and enervation. I realized the importance of some lost attributes like health, wealth and relationships. I realized the right kind of activities meant for me, the right group I belong to, a prominent direction that paved my future path waiting for me. I would always be thankful and grateful to my friends and my mentors who not only supported me but also stood by me.

The most important realization that I was made aware of and learnt in this phase was the values that I already possessed and just needed to polish. It was the value of the inner potential. I found solace in books which not only helped me to increase my knowledge but also to develop as an individual. Introspection not only helped me overcome the negativities but also helped me to relax my mind. As if I had discovered a new me in this crisis. The most peaceful person in the world is the one who has faced and fought the hardest portion of his survival battle and has always emerged as a winner. When we lose all hope, it is the leader within us which holds forth that single ray and brightens our present and future. Rough days should be remembered, lessons should be learnt, and the leader within us should be awakened. They shape our lives and when tackled with positive approach the outcome is a bright one. It is only possible if the lessons are applied effectively and with complete responsibility.

"The toughest situation awakens the leader within us"

Leadership through mentorship:

Every human being is a leader, but this should be awakened at some point of time. Leadership qualities and all business skills can be learnt, but in a different manner. We think we can learn about these qualities by following someone in a group, or admiring a person, but the most important person who can polish this quality is our own self. Instead of finding a leader in a group, why not awaken the same within us through right mentorship. A single training session and mentorship can provoke the leader within and show us direction. This is something which needs to be practiced and taught. Having the right mentor and a loyal friend is a symbol of living in a perfect leadership environment. Everyone has leadership qualities, but mentorship gives shape to these qualities – it pushes, activates and forces the quality to come out and act on a right direction.

The most effective and quick way to achieve the "Real want" is to approach a worthy, proven, guide – a mentor, who has himself crossed the path you are exploring. What cannot be achieved by a strong lecture, study of relevant topics, is easily obtained in the company of such a mentor. Just as sun produces light, which all the stars put together can't give – the mentor alone imparts all the dimensions of knowledge to reach the "Real want". His movements and words give us "silent" advice.

A mentor is a person who:

- Helps you be on the track to achieve your "real want"
- Helps you realize your potential for optimal utilization.
- Helps you to lead yourself and lead by examples.
- Inspires you consistently to walk one step forward, rather than standing still at one place.

The virtue of forgiveness, being ego-less, ability to inspire, control of mind and benevolence are found in a mentor– whose guidance continues to inspire and motivate even in his absence. Mentoring is an interaction in which not only do I choose my mentor but also where my mentor chooses me – it's always a two- way process. They could be anyone amongst your parent, sibling, a professor, any business leader, a spiritual leader, or anybody whom you could relate and follow. If you have decided to achieve something new which you have never achieved before, then you have to go through a transition that you've never had before. A mentor is the right guide, a catalyst who guides and gives the right direction to receive oneself to achieve something different.

A great human converts into a great leader: (The SHC formula)

Gratitude is another crucial characteristic of a great leader. A human-being can become a great leader. People follow some ground yet basic rules to lead their life – the principles of success. We all come across many people in our day-to-day life – some good, some bad, and some who are different from the lot; they leave a mark on your mind forever – we intend to follow them, be like them, and replicate them. Intense gratifications await them who light up a direction in our life – great humanity is always noticed with a fire to makes others successful. The same drew a mark on me, when I came across an uncle – who was humane, had benevolence and epitome of values. He was not so close to me as he was to my parents. I have immense respect for him and will always be grateful for his teachings.

This incident which is surrounded with real life education, goes back to the time when I was only 13-years-old. It is very close to my heart and I am very sure that most of you will relate it with your personal life. We are all aware how cricket crazy we are as a nation. Like all I too had the cricket fever from a very early age. I would spend all my time playing cricket. It had become one of the most important activities in my daily routine which I couldn't miss anyhow. I would finish school work in a hurry and would look forward to going back to the field every day. Like most families where sports were not well accepted as a part of our future, my parents too were worried about my craze for the sports. They thought that I would give up my studies for the game, which was not the truth, and I couldn't explain it to them as I was too young. To put a stop to my inclinations towards cricket, my father decided to hire a tutor at home, to fill in the time that I had already dedicated to cricket. It was tough for me but I was left with no choice but to give up my dedicated play hours to the new routine set for me.

My passion for the sport was so strong, that without thinking about the consequences; I directly headed towards the field without informing anyone. When I returned home around eight in the evening, I saw my father waiting for me. Furious at such careless behavior, he scolded me and tagged me irresponsible. This went on for more than half an hour. I heard him going out silently. After a while my uncle joined us for a dinner. When he heard about the incident that happened in the evening, instead of shouting he took me aside, and explained to me personally. Our conversation changed my attitude towards life completely. He spoke about the importance of studies and he also explained the reason behind the restrictions from my father. At the end of the conversation I understood the importance of my life and the decisions I make. I will never forget all that he had shared with me that day. Of the entire conversation one very basic idea is the one I still remember. Life is based on some principles and values which we need to follow, and the three most important ones are "sincerity, honesty and continuity" (SHC).

We all have these qualities in us; it is only that we do not continuously implement and follow it. Being sincere towards your "Real want" in your life, being honest to yourself, your parents and everyone around you, and most importantly maintaining consistency in your work are signs of being a good leader. From that day onwards, whenever and wherever applicable I tried to implement it. We all follow some or the other formulas in our lives, I call it is SHC formula – being sincere, honest and maintaining continuity in our work, This SHC formula helps us to mould into a great human and thus a great leader. I still remember at that time, my uncle worked for a transport company for an amount of two thousand rupees per month. Today he is not only a successful person but has made dozens of people successful. He is now an owner of the most trusted transport and supplier's business in his state. Later; he has also diversified into machinery, civil, construction and industrial engineering. Today he is a big name, has earned fame and a lot of happiness in his life. It verifies that he has always maintained great leadership towards his work.

"A good human being is always a good leader"

Better your relation, better your leadership:

Human being survives due to the environmental existence - the society we live in within which we share our relationships. Every relationship has an impact in our lives. Our life is clearly viewed and can be understood based on the relationships we share – with our family, friends, mentors, and soul mates. I started business at a very age of 18 - my work was to sell e-learning computer products. The purpose of starting a business along with my close friends was to earn some money. The vision was limited to earn some pocket money to have a good life style – have a congenial tender age, plan for a short exotic trip, have some five star dinners, and if possible, to own a luxury bike. The inherent tendency of being sincere and dedicated towards whatever I did too continued in the series of my business, but often I found it difficult for my friends to share the same attitude – the attitude to take the business seriously in a long- term perception. However, as a group of close-knit friends, we kept on with the business activities. "Prospecting for new customers" to "presenting them our products", "closing the sales" to "training the new joining associates" were our daily activities. We put in arduous work and learnt the business process from the base. The relation we shared with each other became more meaningful – we started valuing our dreams, personal time and individual victory, our focus was to help each other. In the meantime, all of us experienced that "leadership" is a term which one need to prove it in his personal life and relationship is the basic ingredient to make it happen.

We had nothing at the start of the mission – the mission to be financially independent by the early age of twenties. But very soon within a year, we entered the elite group – we could feel our changing lifestyle, we started earning per week, we were called successful by other fellow friends. It gave us immense satisfaction that we were independent. Hence, I kept challenging myself. For every prosperity and achievement, we gained, can be credited to the relationship we shared, the collective effort we put in and the moments we all dreamt big.

Unfortunately, due to occurrence of unavoidable circumstances

– delusion, ego clashes, flounder, interference between personal and professional life, we had differences amongst ourselves. Within a few months, it began to affect our business. We started facing turbulence due to the lack of focus in maintaining our relationship. Most of the team partners were not able to accept each other. This, in turn, resulted in the lack of vision, our collective focus got disturbed, our sales went low, the graph took a downward slope, and existing customers started complaining about services, the efficiency was hampered and so on. The business dropped and the friends parted ways; at the end, it was only one of my childhood friends who stood by me and we decided to start all over again.

The business got refreshed from the scratch. We started it again – approached our prospective customers, presented our products, follow up, trainings, closing the sales. Twenty-four hours a day, seven days a week, our thoughts were only prioritizing to make the business successful – achieve all the lost ones. New people came onboard, new talent and potential, and with immense hard work we again conquered what we had lost. In the entire process of restarting and restructuring my lost business all over again, my dedication had to pay for losing a special relationship. The negligence towards the same hampered my personal life to such an extent that it disturbed me personally leading me to suffer severe depression. This not only affected my mindset but also drastically hampered my professional career.

The most important lesson in this period was to "accept the people the way they are" and "keep a balance between the professional and personal relationship". This is the root cause of a healthy leadership existence. We generally tend to focus on our professional life so much that we tend to ignore our personal life. We cannot succeed or be a leader without keeping personal relationships intact. It is the people who are close to us, our pillar of support, and our strength. Being in this busy society, the intension of achieving personal success, competing ourselves always keeps on focusing to have our success. These channelize our time to give commitment to our professional action plans, sacrificing the personal relationships. Maintaining relationship always implies an effective leadership. The truth lies in our lives which is a mirror of the relationships we share. People need people to succeed. A strong bondage with another person gives a meaningful relationship. This creates a common goal, consistent purpose, strengthens learning curve and increases the confidence to act. The combined efforts are channelized towards the same common output which amplifies the success. Maintaining simplicity, being grounded, understanding and accepting people they are, always remain in the quadrant of building a solid relationship – personal, professional, and social.

Leadership is about giving your best:

Giving your best in all aspects of the life is the other name to leadership. Whatever we do, we have to give our best. Let us imagine that each one of us, every human being would start realizing the unlimited capabilities and potential within them. What would be the impact if every individual would not only find the leader within, but also implement its potential? It is we who have to take the step in creating an environment and follow it as a culture where every individual applies his leadership qualities and gives their best in their respective field. Then surely the place that we live in would be a better place, with the best opportunities and we will be the reason for a new and advanced world.

Success does not come free of cost. We have to pay a fee in terms of hard work, efforts and commitment. If we continue to work with commitment and dedication, it will result in an environment of the best performers doing their best. This in turn helps improve society and the nation, leading to a nation of super power, not only in the sense of its economy, but also in the sense of values and leadership.

When one's real want is encountered, and implemented with the strength of self-belief, applied with a meaningful attitude, then understanding the leader within is the prime factor which makes one successful. Truly it's not how one person becomes successful, rather it is the depth of understanding a personal leader within us, which adds to the reasons that makes others to follow. Your achievements and benchmarks should inspire people to go ahead, and for that you have to be a successful figure.

Summary

- Leadership is not about getting the best out of everything, but about managing to do the extraordinary out of nothing.
- Certain family lessons can sometimes help to make you unique.
- A leader is always available in your family.
- A strong leader will do the best in the relevant field and create an example for the society.
- Leadership is not about position, but about the ability to take initiative and the sense of responsibility that one takes.
- A great human has the potential to be a great leader.
- The SHC formula of leadership is being sincere to your dream, honest to your elders and maintaining continuous effort.

Invisible leader – Self answered section:

- Narrate any three situations from your life, where you feel you have given your best. Visualize the situations and list all the learning's you gained from it.
- Find out a leader from your family, accept that person as one of your mentors and start emulating him/her.

7

Thinking beyond the Reach

"The mind is what the mind is fed"
–David J. Schwartz

We are all blessed with a sensible mind. Our mind which is filled with various thoughts that are sometimes positive, negative and sometimes ambitious. These thoughts are indeed our guides to achieve success in life. It provides a path, creates clarity in what we want, and helps in manifestation. People restrict accepting the clarity in their thoughts, and their capabilities to act. By broadening our horizons, we open ourselves to the world full of opportunities and ways to achieve success at a different level. In our society, we have different people who come from diverse backgrounds and cultures. If we explore lives of people who are rich and famous, we will see that they were initially part of less fortunate people. They took all the possible efforts to extend their thoughts and implement without restricting their imagination and confidence. We all are accomplished with equally good livese with numerous opportunities but everything is interpreted with the status of mindset and the reach of our thinking intensity.

You are the primary reason of your failure, dissatisfaction and sorrows. You are the only source that can attract all negative and positive forces to your life. Your thoughts, feelings and particularly your mindset define your existence. There are many success stories about people who started with a fraction of asset with them and with determination and practice became excellent leaders. They have transited from being a "part of crowd" to be a "reason for the crowd". They have challenged their own level of thinking and benchmarked a new stage for the society. History has proved that higher the level of thinking, higher is the level of success and therefore the true satisfaction.

"Primarily it's not one's talent, but "thinking" that creates success"

It was the year 2007. Our city had the opportunity to host one of the most prestigious seminars for the first time in so many years. My childhood friend, Ramprasad had invited me to join him for the same. I had no idea about it at all. The events that would be held, the speakers invited, how it would elevate my engineering career, I was totally clueless. Yet I agreed to join him not only because we were childhood buddies and he was a confidant but at the same time I had received an opportunity to attend a corporate seminar. I was super excited and awaited eagerly for the day.

The 14th of January had finally arrived. It was around 8:30 am when suddenly there was a knock at my door. I was attired in a casual outfit, and was preparing to leave for the venue. As soon as I opened the door, Ramprasad stood there to pick me and brief me a little about the event to be attended. He was attired in a complete business suit. Dazzled by his formal outfit I too decided to wear the same. On our way towards the venue which was approximately 10 kms. from the starting point, Ramprasad briefed me about the event. He described that the event was a youth centric, multi professional and public discussion forum about being highly successful in life. The speaker was a renowned youth entrepreneur and a huge crowd was expected. My excitement doubled as I was going to meet a successful youth entrepreneur and would be able to learn the secrets of starting a business early in my life. My dream was coming true.

We reached the venue half an hour before the event started. I was equally nervous and excited about the event. My intention was to grasp a lot of knowledge and fundamentals about the secrets of being successful. As expected, present there was long queue of young, well dressed, mostly professional but students. They had come from all across the country which included students from IIT Kharagpur, to name a few. I was curious about the speaker, who could draw such a crowd? When we finally entered, his entry was nothing less than that of a celebrity with hundreds cheering him. Most of the people knew him before I was introduced. When he entered the stage, he seemed unbelievable – his personality, looks, style was comparable to celebrity and a positive aura spoke volumes about him. It was a three-hour interactive presentation session about a business plan and some e -literacy products. While I heard, him give the presentation, I was totally impressed with his persona and the positive vibes that flew across the auditorium.

Prior to the meeting I thought the speaker would be middle-aged, but it was a real surprise when I came to know that, he was a 2nd year engineering student at one of the IITs. At the age of 20, he was a self-made millionaire with a huge fan following across the country. He described his journey to success – his initiative, sacrifices, thought process, strategies he used and the consistency he maintained to become a public figure. I replaced myself with his status and imagined. The feelings were different and so touching. This feeling was sufficient for me to think something beyond my reach and make a benchmark in society.

After the event I was overwhelmed with the positivity and was expressing my gratitude to Ramprasad for inviting me to his wonderful inspiring event which gave me an idea to set my benchmark for my future. My thinking and mindset went toa different level – if a person of my age can do this, it is possible for me as well to reach the heights of success. I was into 1st year of engineering and there is a nominal difference in our age but he was a self-made millionaire. I thought, "why not me too?".

While I was deep in certain positive thoughts, I would see a bunch of youngsters' rush to him for autographs and some others discussing about their view in groups.

Someone remarked, "How can a youngster be so popular at

such a tender age, and have such a huge fan following, self-made millionaire, youth reorganization – it's impossible, it must be a false projection.

Another said, "It's not possible that everybody will have the same success, might be it was his luck and had a good education background to showcase"

We both heard the remarks made by the general crowd. Although the speaker fascinated me, these remarked left me a little confused when Ramprasad justified them saying, "In a crowd of hundreds of people, especially youth, such criticism is common. These are emotions, suggestions and interpretations made by humans. When we talk about success (he continued), people are not measured by their height, complexions, their parents, background they came from, age group they belong to or their college degree. They are measured by their achievements – it's the result that counts not the depth of efforts. The way a person can think, the highest level a person can think effectively; do make him different in the crowd. People respect people due to their behavior, which is directly translated from their thought process and the level of thinking they have".

I was mesmerized by the event and the conversation we had. From that instance, I never dreamt of small things or stooped low in my thoughts about my future.

"Don't ever stop yourself from thinking you can"

It's a general awareness that expanding our "thinking process" is always beneficial. We all target to be successful, but all of us are not able to achieve it. The reason behind having very few people who claim success is because they think differently. Some people term it as high thinking, big thinking, and extraordinary thinking, but at the end it is a process of "thinking beyond the reach" – it's about challenging what exists and benchmarking a new success for the rest to follow. Only a few of us can "think beyond their reach", why? I have asked my friends, mentors, acquaintances and myself as well. The success we achieve today is because of the thoughts and the set benchmarks for us, we had in the past and the thinking we carry today will manifest in our future as success or failure. Many people are not able to "think beyond the reach" because of reasons like:

1. Thought Paralysis:

Our actions follow the way we think and it determines our lives. People tend to restrict their thinking and their thought direction which get paralyzed to think beyond thus their action too stops. They are satisfied with the smaller achievements they have in their lives and consider themselves as failures for not being highly successful.

"If they don't think, they don't act and they don't achieve"

2. Fear of criticism:

What people will think about me, when I will talk about something extraordinary? It's a general question that comes to mind and it is the fear of being criticized. What will happen if they will fail to achieve what they had set out for? It stops the majority from talking about something big and extraordinary.

"They don't talk big, they don't think big, they don't act and they don't achieve big"

3. Believe scarcity:

Every person has different potential and competencies; however, there are a few people who have the potential and capabilities but do not use them. They tend to believe that since they belong to an environment of non-achievers they too cannot achieve anything. People underestimate themselves and do not believe in their own potentials. This puts a full stop to their belief system and they remain away from their Real Want.

"They don't believe, they don't talk big, they don't think big, they don't act big and thus they don't achieve anything big"

4. Luck dominance:

A human mind always receives what it observes from the society. When a person sees a luxury, car passing by, sees a big house, meets some positive personalities, or any positive relations, they create feelings of positive for all those. If others can achieve and live their dreams, we could do it; I can also live my dream. These people observe, feel, learn and act to achieve their dreams.

They stop being in the class of mediocre and start thinking big to achieve big. Some people think negative; to them another's success seems like an act of luck rather than the result of determination and hard work along with positive thinking. It's particularly luck that dominates in any success story. So they feel they cannot succeed since they have neither the luck nor the capability.

"Resistance to think beyond reach"

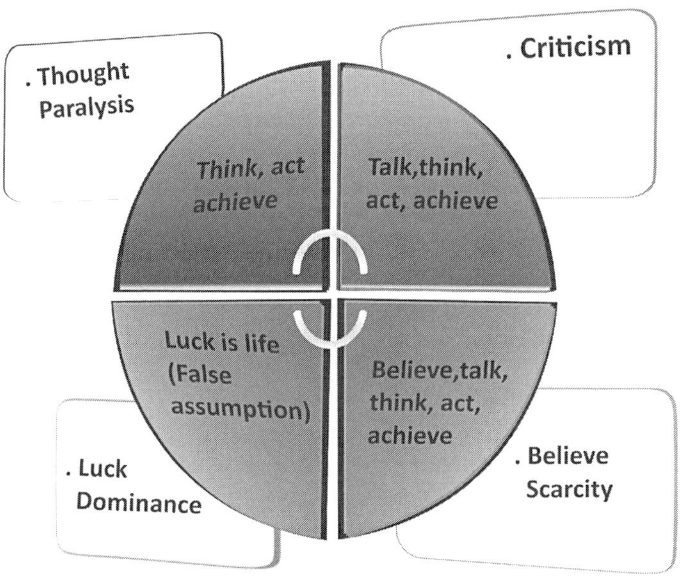

Everything starts from a thought:

In one of my personal surveys of people from different background and professions, I realized one hidden truth of the human mind. I had asked some simple questions to the interviewees. One of them being, "What is your weakness that you want to overcome?" I got different answers such as bad communication, leadership skills, inability to maintain relationships, lack of writing skills, procrastination, etc. Interestingly, most response from more than 40% of the people was "I don't have any weakness" I was surprised for it is impossible "Not to have any weakness".

There is always an area where a person needs to develop, grow and adopt change. From the category of people with "No weakness", it is understood that the biggest weakness of these people is "the inability to think big". Since they are not able to think big, they cease to think that they are not big. People think they know everything and can face every situation but at the end of the day these so called "No weakness" people fail drastically. Everything starts with a thought and the ability to think big.

In one of my training session five years back I was asked. Who is the first person to land on the moon? Confidently I answered, "Neil Armstrong". From a corner a voice said: No! That's the wrong answer. I was shocked and challenged him. The answer was a masterpiece. It was not Neil Armstrong, rather his thought that first reached the moon. The answer was brilliant and in its simplicity. Our thought drags us to our achievement. The thought triggers before the action takes place. As you think so you achieve. It's you who can decide your thoughts and the level of thinking.

Feel big to think big:

The best way to think big is to feel big. The process of achieving starts from feeling good about your future achievement. To achieve big things in your life, you have to do big things, act big and it initiates from feeling good. Your feelings are associated with what you talk. Talking something big leads to the desire for big achievements and in turn it converts to a feel-good factor. In our general society people are categorized based on what they talk:

- People who admire other's work (these are small minds who talk only about people)
- People who admire and discuss with others about the positivity learnt from them (these are average minds who talk

about certain events)

- People who inspire others by their activities, so that they can be admired by others (these are big minds who talk about ideas)

The moot point is; you must decide your own category from the above you want to position yourself. When you think, and talk about an important thing, you create a picture or images in your mind. Let's say that you are telling your friends "I want to buy a Maruti Alto" simultaneously you create image of the vehicle in your mind. If you convert your mind to saying, "I want to buy a BMW 5 series" then you also simultaneously create an image of the model, color and series of that car in your mind. When you create those images, a feeling of happiness is created. This is where the game changes. When you feel good about images consistently, that manifests in your life.

You should be successful because "People should think high when they think about you". Need, want, results and achievements are a never-ending process. A new prominent level of benchmark can be set and can be achieved by achieving something high in our society. You must be successful because there's a next big thing waiting for you. Your trend of **"Thinking big"**, working for it and achieving it should make the audiences think big. Every success story starts with proper intention and your influential intention will inspire others to think big and for that you must be a successful figure.

Summary

- Primarily it's not one's talent, but the thinking that create success.
- Higher the level of your thinking, higher is the level of the achievement in each aspect of life.
- The success we have today is due to the thinking we have had in our past.
- "They don't believe, they don't talk big, they don't think big, they don't act big and thus they don't achieve anything big"
- Belief and being consistent is the key to achieving the dream.
- Many people are not able to think big because they stop themselves from doing so.
- Ignoring to think big is like the situation you are in.
- As you think and feel, so you achieve

Thinking beyond the reach: Self-answered section

- Identify three priority areas of your life and find out what can be the best benchmarks you can create in each of the areas. (Areas could be in education, business, relationship, societal etc. Try to find out what best can be done in these areas mapped with your potential and resources).

8

A Positive Failure

"Failure is the only opportunity to begin again more intelligently"
– Henry Ford

Behind every success story, there is disappointment, too much effort, a stumble, a setback or a radical tilt of direction. Choosing to be successful throughout the rest of your life and enjoying meaningful success, where life is full of happiness and making a difference is what an individual demands . The hidden opportunity, reason for growth, the pride of owning the throne, and the happiness of success are all at the base of failures. Understanding failures and the section of implementation required is the fraction which plays a vital role in the journey of success.

The word "failure" itself is enough to stop someone from goingahead with their plans. Majority of them simply wind up, turn around, and accept their failure without trying. The optimum probability of succeeding or being labeled as "successful" is almost a mythical pursuit. The lessons taught by legends like Columbus, Graham Bell, Woolworth, Edison, The Wright Brothers, Henry Ford,

Dhirubhai Ambani, Mahatma Gandhi to name a few, makes us realize that they could perceive the world with a difference. Although they failed, but they never gave up. Most stories about these personalities have demonstrated and taught us that they were successful because they appreciated their failures.

This concept has always stretched my thoughts reminding me my sales career days when I suffered a common speech defect. The past journey has always been a conducive one and it was always because of my "failure", irrespective of its dimensions and severity. (A profession where interaction within customers is maximum, conveying the features of products and connecting customers an effective speech plays the most prominent role) I was supposed

to give presentations on the products, and at the initial stage "my ineffective speech" was my hindrance. I still remember the days when people used to tease me and bully me because of my stammering defect. My colleagues and prospects would get bored during my presentations, and friends would get up from their seats in the middle of a presentation and close my mouth or interrupt the presentation. They would jeer me saying, "First learn to speak and then deliver your presentation."

Someone with a similar experience could relate to the amount of pressure that used to build on me at that point of time. This was not just once. It continued for years, ever since I was at school. I was bullied, teased and made fun of. From school to graduation, until my professional life started. Each day was a fresh day for me but with the same results. Somehow or the other I promised myself that I will overcome this shortcoming and I am proud that I did. The feeling of defeat was always triggering me to stretch my potential to the best, prove myself and feel the moments of success.

Each day I used to go to my prospect's doorstep to promote my computer education products. After giving hundreds of presentations to more than a hundred people I could sell my first package. I was offering products which were perfect in all aspects

– good features, user-friendly and value for money as well. I had conviction in my products and was sure they would be helpful to all whom I was presenting. After all this, the answer after every presentation was a resolute "No". Often my mind would conceive only negative thoughts which were a big hindrance for me to convert all those temporary results to a gratifying achievement. At that time, it was quite natural for society to label me as a "failure". I would motivate myself saying, "Maybe I am a failure, but not a quitter". Gathering countless No's from my prospects was an opportunity to convert those into "Yes". It was truly the most extreme learning experience for me. After getting innumerable negative responses I kept trying and the lessons from each failure were unique.

The rejection from the general crowd had always been an attribute to change myself – find out the core fault. I usually refused to react or argue about the same. Instead I started pointing out and asking myself. "Why is this happening to me? Where am I lacking? What is pulling me back?" I started to jot down all the mistakes I did throughout the day. At night, I would analyze and work upon them. Analysis was the most crucial factor that helped me get over the problem and finally earn me recognition as the "best inspiring youth" at the end of the engineering course. The process I went through to reach this position was a lesson. Failure is always due to the absence of competency to perform in the face of a challenge but being a failure can be an impressive way to learn and amusingly provide the means for life's immense discovery and success.

Try to discover:

Being a failure is not the end. It is completely your decision whether to give up and repent for the rest of the life or to overcome the obstacles and try until you succeed. Once you decide to be successful you will surely face failure. Instead, failure should be treated as the first step towards success. Every time you fail, instead of getting disappointed, convince yourself that you will rise to win. There is a misperception about the difference between what one can change and one who refrains from the possible change. Personal growth, the directions to climb up, and the process of discovering oneself often remain under the shade.

Intense criticisms and social rejectioninstigatedme to work hard on my speech problems. After returning home at night I analyzed the reasons for stammering. The doctor's diagnosis stated a slight irregular length of the tongue. My passion for physics encouraged me to learn more about the problem related to sounds and how these are created. I learnt phonology and how it is related to human biological systems - the study of vocal cords, its sync with tongue, sound creation and the response of ear drums. The control over the momentum of tongue and its rhythm always maintains a good speech – I discovered that. I practiced the art of controlling my tongue momentum and synchronized it with the contents of what I was speaking. With a strong preparation, I started presenting to my prospects in an unusual way but failures were never-ending. I was rejected but I enjoyed discovering myself throughout the process of rejection. It took some time to overcome the situation but what I learnt, I started penning down those lessons and began to implement my learning over subsequent presentations. I was surprised to see the results after some months – it was unbelievable, the negativity turned to positivity, rejections were converted to acceptance, criticisms transited into appreciation. The significant point is not about the results that I achieved, but it was the satisfaction after the achievement. At a certain situation, the confidence and experience I earned were hundred times valuable than the results I received.

Failure is not the result of bad luck rather it occurs due to our mistakes. It is us who can understand why we failed and discover the unnoticed potential within us. These experiences are simple and directive; they show us how we need to correct ourselves. The lessons and learning may not give you instant success, but these can adjust your thoughts and actions to achieve it in the future. This is the concept which remains uniform in nature and applies to all sorts of failures irrespective of its level and magnitude.

The real failure is not when you fail, but when you ignore the learnings from it. Discovering you, finding out the unnoticed factor with an open intention and understanding the nature's response at the same time will align your thoughts in a productive direction. A short-term failure is a symbol from the universe; it is the way in which the universe tries to inform us that we are not heading towards the right direction – our intentions and activities are mismatched and we are moving in an undesired direction. If we are practically intelligent to accept those signals, then surely a different direction will come out for us to achieve "The Real Want".

Respect the failure:

Failure is a mirror for your action. The reflections from it are the evidence of the potential you carry. The thing that can make you head towards "the real want" are the lessons from past mistakes. It makes you question yourself, ask, who you are in the real world? What is your potential? What can you do in real life? What is your status and standard? The reality of the progress in life comes from these failures. Accepting the mistakes with respect provides a reason to learn from them. A transition in the mindset, development in behavior, understanding what works for an individual and what not, are all hidden within the degree of acceptance of the mistakes we did. The lessons learnt from the mistakes, which when implemented leads to a self-growth – an inner development.

Each human is a gift of the universe that one should believe from the core. Everyone is born with a unique quality. Realizing the potential and giving a shape to it is always needed. I have seen many of my friends who have been pampered by their parents since childhood. When they were exposed to the real world, they were shocked by the response they got. The real world was full of commitments, challenges, struggle and failures. Many people who are not exposed to failures become egoist – they think themselves as superior to others. Most of the times these so-called 'lucky people' are a 'big zero' in their real life.

To try something new and fail is not failure. Acquiring new skill and brushing as individual requires us to enter unexplored arenas that can provide us with new knowledge and potentials. Expecting to learn something new without failure, might lead to an unpleasant shock. Had you not fallen off from your cycle in your childhood, would you learn how to ride a cycle? Failure taught you to ride the cycle. That time you respected your failure and tried to achieve "The real want" – to ride a bicycle. The continuous process to learn and grow helped you achieve this want. Self-respect and inner realization will help change your situation instead of listening to how others want you to behave. Thus, it's a positive failure.

Failure – a gateway towards the "real want". It connects an individual's potential and their achievement. Your failure shouldn't hide your real want; instead, it should make your task easier and allow you to choose the right direction towards your "Real want" provided you have learnt the necessary lessons. Making a mistake is not a crime; not learning from them and repeating them is a crime. Only a fool will do so.

What makes you fail?

The outer circumstances play a minor fraction in the role of failure, but our inner world contributes to a major portion in our failure. Nobody can destroy their image, but their own mindset can. Certain inner attributes and our personal reaction towards our practical life make a difference in our success graph.

Faith:

Even after presence of numerous solutions and a path to follow; people fail, due to the lack of faith. The lack of faith within the work they do, the system they are associated with, and even a constant doubt on personal ability leads to dilution of enthusiasm and passion to act. The absence of faith decreases the confidence and enforces blame on others. People blame others for every fault. "Nothing is my fault; everything happened because of someone else or something else" – one says.

Lack of faith

↓

Blaming others

↓

Failure

The constant activity of blaming others becomes a habit. Blaming others for one's own cause creates a very negative environment and thus the disturbed mindset leads to failure.

Attitude:

Existence of an unfamiliar situation, delay in the expectation, cloudy intentions etc. are quite natural. The abnormal lies in the way we react to these situations. It can be based on either of the issues:

- Your patience when you don't have anything.
- Your attitude and reaction when you have everything

Improper attitude

Distractions

Failure

An improper attitude misleads a direction causing a distraction in the action plans and thus reaches an unexpected failure.

Ignorance:

Ignoring new things to learn, forgetting the mistakes done and resistingchange as per the demand of the situation, keeps us away from the current updates and becomes a blockage for the wisdom we could receive.

Ignorance

Blockage

Misinterpretation

Ineffective decision

Failure

These blockages tilt our mindset in misinterpreting the situation we are in. Understanding the situation wrongly binds us to take an ineffective decision and these results in a foolish failure.

Loyal:

Not being loyal towards your "Real want" will dilute the value of your dream – the significance vanishes. Wanting something in your life sets a concrete expectation and which when not able to achieve, creates a fear within, which overshadows the "Real Want".

Not being loyal

↓

Fear

↓

Overshadow Real want

↓

inappropriate direction

↓

Failure

The passion to achieve the real want will help build up everything again. The power of the feeling of achievement of the real want, and the lessons learnt from life can restructure a new direction. Many people quit after the first failure in spite of having a clear reason to achieve the Real Want, because of inability to restructure their plan. People develop an inappropriate direction which takes one to an unintentional destination labeling as a failure.

Unity & Relationship:

An appropriate direction is the primary solution from coming out of all the distractions, dissatisfaction and failure. The solution which are not delivered from within, are always received from our outside world – be it friends, family, loved ones, professional circle, community we belong to and also from the ones we hate. Relating to society and maintaining unity leads to a successful environment.

Not being united

↓

Breaks out relationship

↓

Solution Breakage

↓

Failure

Not being united with the society we live in, keeps us away from the valuable solutions which are based on other people's pocket. This separates us from the society and results in a breakdown of healthy relationships. A breakage in this cycle leads to an undesirable failure.

Egoistic:

The most egoistic people belong to the category who find it difficult to be successful. They reject most solutions, ideas and people and thus they are rejected by society one day. This rejection keeps them away from the solutions and the possible lessons that life teaches us and they end up with situational failure.

Ego

↓

Rejects a lot

↓

Away from solution

↓

Failure

The above points highlight the reasons of one's failure which is very individualistic in nature. People fail because of their own, but they become successful when they learn from the rejections and the oppositions they face. People want to face something new, uneven, and challenging and keep growing. It becomes a reason for all successful people to relate their life with learnings from their failure. Literally it's not about how people become successful, but it's about the intention of learning from failure and implementing at the right time, which ignites them to be successful, because on the way it is failure that teaches how to create history. You must be successful because the story you will share, will inspire the whole world.

Summary

- A successful person has always appreciated their failures.
- Failures can be changed into success by learning from it and achieving self-realization.
- Being a failure is not the end of life, it depends on your decision.
- Failures are directive: they show us how to correct ourselves.
- Learn from your failure and start implementing the lessons.
- Making mistakes is not a crime; repeating the same mistakes are.
- The fear of failure shouldn't dominate "The real want."
- A positive failure is the medium to achieve your "real want."

A positive failure: Self-answered section

- Write down the three big failures you have faced in the last two years.
- Write down the learnings you receivedfrom each of these failures.
- Write down the reasons for your failures and its occurrence clearly.
- What step will you take to utilize the learning.

9

Be a Mirror to Yourself

"Keep your best wishes, close to your heart and watch what happens"

– Tony DeLiso

You studied hard, worked hard, and maintained all your relationships perfectly. As a matter of fact, you are hardworking, obedient, sincere and honest, but at the end of the day what matters is the ultimate result. You worked hard but what if you didn't get any results? What is the use of the challenging work then? Isn't it just a waste? Today's generation believes in the quality of the results than the quantity of the efforts given. Every effort put in the right direction and intention gives rise to two possibilities – either success or failure. If one succeeds, it is time for glory and happiness – to set up new goals. If one faces failure, then instead of being upset, one should still be happy, and try to learn from it to avoid the same mistakes again. The cause of failure, the further changes required and correct implementation are necessary actions. It is the time that will allow you to connect with yourself, introspect, to know your weakness and work upon it.

If you feel that you are doing well, working hard, maintaining all the principles of success, but still you fail, then it is time for you to be a mirror yourself – analyze the mistake. Our image in the mirror doesn't lie. Most people think, feel and believe that they are flawless, but the mirror shows them the reality. Ours mirror is our own heart. The biggest truth is once again the voice of our heart – the mirror for you. You can lie, misbehave, and even forget others, but you can't get away from the voice of your heart. It is something that observes your activities day and night. Your heart responds to activities done by you in the sense of feelings. It is you who decides to listen to your heart or disregard it. It's you who is ready to understand the feelings, welcome the changes, adopt the intelligence and take your life ahead. It's you who is really interested in making an environment pure and satisfactory. It is totally up to you. Some people accept the voice of the heart and start changing whereas some ignore the reality of the inner world and continue to be in the same category.

Life is about YOU:

The most successful people of the world are those who love themselves the most – their values, intentions, decisions and the attitude they carry. They experiment with themselves from each angle and make a brand of themselves. Life itself is a big project. Maintaining our own inner world and applying that in the outer world is a lifetime project. I studied engineering, entrepreneurship, pursued management in international business and simultaneously managed people, money, time, business and myself. I handled lots of projects during my graduation and during my master's. The project started and ended up with limited learning for me as well as the other students. Above all the project of life itself is the parent project with a special purpose - meant and defined differently for all. Each purpose is a huge and lifetime project. It depends on the individual who handles the project what shape it gets. Apart from the support, love and affection of our near and dear ones, we are on our own, the shape life takes depends on how we direct it. The success and failure you have is because of you and your future is purely and solely adjudicated by you. That's why life is called a Do-it-yourself-project.

People keep searching for answers, but the best answers they get are from their own hearts and minds. Life is all about an individual perception. Every person under any circumstances or condition takes help of other people; they can be friends, relatives, neighbors, company partners or associates. They enquire about a lot of things from others and obtain hundreds of solutions. At the end of the day they use the solution which they always wanted to use. Doing work that is close to the heart is always the safest solution. It is your life, your dream, therefore the achievement will be yours, and success is for you. It's obvious that the road to success is to be chosen by you. Nobody else can help you walk. The support and suggestion you get from others will be a part of your learning; your teachers, mentors, parents, elders are only the medium to teach you and guide you. The ultimate decision must be taken by you and the path you chose will direct you towards success. The earlier you realize this, the more quickly you will grow.

Expecting your success from others is simply a waste of time. You know yourself better than others and the answers you give yourself will be genuine and enough strong to act on it. Your mind, heart and potential will synchronize, once you start asking answers to yourself rather than finding them all over the place. The biggest realization is self-realization. Self-realization leads to self-growth and a constant growth leads to success – The Real want.

Many people often wonder why everything goes wrong even when they follow the right direction. Many people have asked me the same question again and again. Their questions can be summarized in a few points.

- I think I have a clear and unambiguous, written goal
- I think I believe in my system, my work and in myself
- I think I have a positive attitude towards everything
- I think I have found a leader within myself
- I think I follow my mentor in the true sense.
- I think big and my thoughts are positive too

When everything is right, why am I not getting all that I want? These categories of people think that they follow every possible principle of success, yet they are not successful. This is because they only think and remain in the state of thinking for the rest of their lives.

- Writing down your dreams is only 50%, rest 50% of the work happens when you start acting on the same.

- Telling that I believe in the system, I believe in myself, and probably thinking about the same reflects only one side of the coin; the reality is on the other side. Belief is not to be told but to be felt. Start feeling the power of the belief.
- Having the right mentor and finding the leader within you is also one side of the coin, applying and implementing that skill and creating something out of nothing is the other side.

It is a general scenario in our college, company or society that most of the people waste 95% of their time in thinking how to utilize the rest 5% of the time resulting in time scarcity. People who think they are right and are doing the right thing. The only difference is they do not act.

The three basic hindrances that stop them from taking action:

1. Not realizing and accepting the Ego within them
2. Not being able to find the key strengths within them
3. Not being able to accept and build relationships.

The society and even the almighty gives us chances to change ourselves and realize our mistakes but if one is not ready to change, the only output reserved for him is "Failure".

"Don't end up only thinking, act on it"

Three things to manage (PMT):

Right from our childhood, the best resources we came across were people, money and time. If we realize our past we can find that, many people helped us in critical situations while money helped us in all aspects of our survival. Time helped in the growing and learning process. The biggest resources an organization or a nation can have are PMT - people, money and time. The optimum utilization of PMT in the best viable way can lead to the best situation in a society and the nation.

In one of the leadership conferences, by a leadership guru, someone from the audience asked him a question. What is that thing, which when managed at a single time, will be able to manage the rest? The answer was – "managing our mind". Once a person can manage his own mind, the rest is managed automatically. Life is a mind game where people, money and time are the key players. One must master the mind game so as to manage the rest of the things.

"Managing your mind, is all about managing PMT"

Managing our mind is all about having the right state of mind throughout the process of work. Failure to maintain will undergo a state of frustration which leads to distraction and sometime disasters. Many a time people don't understand what they want. Not understanding what you want is the prime factor of all distractions. The simple concept to understand "what you want" is to ignore "what you don't want". Start analyzing the activities or things that worry you, irritate you, which create a sense of suffocation. Understanding the activities that you don't want and ignoring them will help you to keep a focus on the activities that you like, you love, feel good about and enjoy the most. This constant focus will create an environment of positivity and the best way to do that is to have a constant focus on the "Real want". The focus converts to intention and intention itself is a power to attract whatever you focus on. The power of the universe, intention, and thoughts are something that exactly maintain balance in the universe.

Being your own mirror is a process of self-growth. People should see you as an idol. They should follow you, learn from you and make you as their mentor. For that, you must be successful and constantly become a **"Mirror for yourself"**, grow consistently and create records by achieving your "Real Want"

Summary

- The most important mirror for one's life is his heart
- Life is a "do–it-yourself" project
- You are the answer for everything
- 3 mistakes generally people do: Don't end up thinking, rather act on it.
- Top 3 things to manage: Managing our mind is all about managing PMT

Be a mirror for yourself: Self-answered section

- List down five activities that always worry you
- Point out one area of your life, where you should be known in your society.

Other #SMBooks

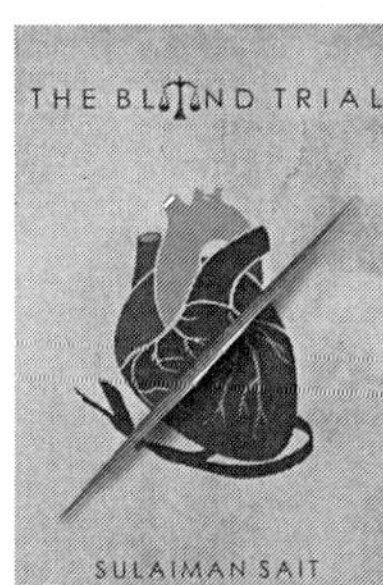

Other #SMBooks

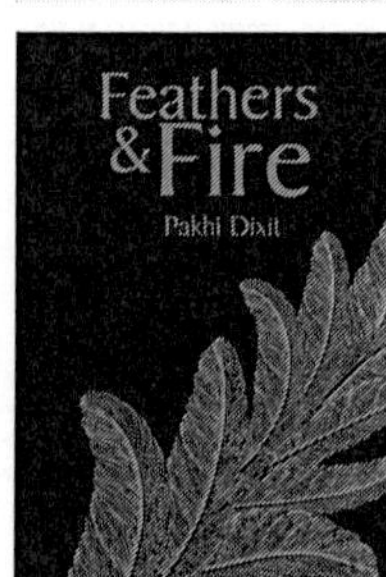